Hard Lying

Hard Lying

An Intelligence Officer
on the Levantine Shore 1914–19

LEWEN WELDON

with an afterword by Barnaby Rogerson

ELAND
London

This edition first published by Eland Publishing Ltd,
61 Exmouth Market, London EC1R 4QL in 2023

ISBN: 978 1 78060 199 1

Cover Image: *Damascus and the Lebanon Mountains from 10,000
Feet* by Richard C. Carline © Imperial War Museum (IWM 3082)

Contents

Foreword

THIS WORK IS MERELY the contents of a diary kept by me from 1914–1915, and so naturally there appears to be only one person of any importance in it, viz. 'LBW'. I can assure my readers, however, that this is not the case. If only the men I had the honour to serve with had kept diaries they would be of far more interest than mine.

There is, however, one person who merits all and more than he was awarded, Lieutenant-Commander Alan Cain, RNR, DSC, who was Captain of HMY *Managem* from 1917–1919.

When I mention in my diary how I went ashore on dark nights in a boat from the *Managem* while lying off a hostile coast, I should also call the attention of my readers to the seamanship and clever navigation required to bring the *Managem* to a correct position off a coast bereft of lights and in many cases badly charted: this, however, was successfully accomplished by Captain Cain on every occasion during the two years I was in his ship.

In connection with this work I must also mention Lt R. Gaskell, RNR, Captain of *Aenne Rickmers*; Lt-Cdr John Kerr, RNR, DSC, of HMS *Anne*; Lt-Cdr S. B. Smith, RNR, DSC, Captain of HMT *Veresis*; Lt-Cdr Morewood, RNR, who commanded HMY *Managem* during the first six months of her commission: and Lt-Cdr Shotton, RNR, Captain of HMS *Devany*.

The difficulties under which they worked can only be fully appreciated by 'those who go down to the sea in ships'.

I would also like to pay a tribute to the great tact shown by these officers during their most difficult commands, in the treatment of my brother officers (both French and British) and myself, and our weird mixture of 'agents'.

LBW

Note 'Hard Lying' is a term applied to a special allowance granted to men serving in small craft, such as destroyers, torpedo-boats, trawlers, etc.

The Eastern

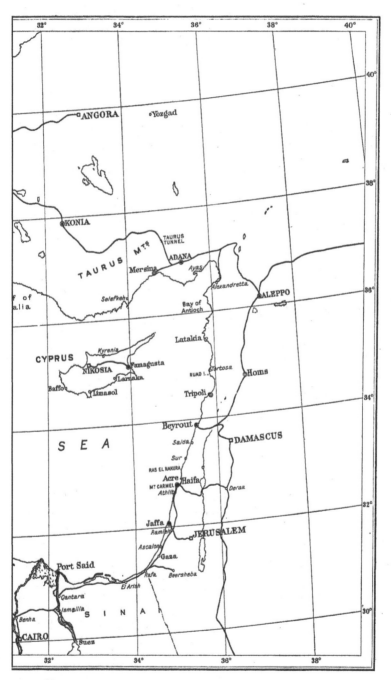

Mediterranean

1

First Months

August, 1914–January, 1915

THE BRITISH DECLARATION of war found me at Marseilles. For just over fourteen years I had been in the service of the Egyptian Government, in the Survey Department, and I was on my way home for my usual biennial leave. Naturally ever since the *Worcestershire* (Bibby Line) left Port Said all of us passengers had been busy discussing the international situation, and the unanimous opinion on board was that we should never be able to hold up our heads again if we did not back up the French – materially as well as with words. Most of us took it as a matter of course that England should throw her weight into the struggle, but we had a particular reason for wanting to know the exact moment at which she was likely to do so. For the *Goeben* and *Breslau* were both cruising in our direct road and we knew it.

We arrived, however, at Marseilles without mishap and picked up our pilot, who informed us – quite erroneously – that both France and England were at war with Germany and that HMS *Suffolk* had sunk several German liners in the Atlantic. But the burst of enthusiasm with which these rumours were greeted was short-lived. Once alongside the quay the true facts of the case were quickly apparent. The French were fighting right enough, but England was still hesitant, and we were made to feel it too. The barges from which we had intended to coal and which were lying ready near us were suddenly towed away again, and I was told by our Captain that we were to be given no facilities of that kind unless England joined forces with France. A minor form of blackmail.

13

Shortly after this incident most of the passengers left the ship to visit the town. As I was walking up the famous Rue Cannebière I was more than once greeted with the contemptuous remark of 'anglais'. The tone in which this was invariably said left no doubt as to what the French were thinking of us at the moment. Decidedly we had not entered the war.

But the next day – 4th August – things were changed indeed, as I was very soon made to understand. The cabman who drove me from the quay into the town absolutely refused to take his six-franc fare. Instead, he stood up in the box, took off his hat and shouted '*Vive l'Angleterre*' at the top of his voice. I was so overcome that I went into the nearest café and called for a Bock. But when I was about to pay the waiter I felt myself tapped on the shoulder, and turned round to face a bearded Frenchman who, with his hat in his hand, was murmuring, '*Non, non, avec moi, Monsieur.*' Most certainly we had entered the war. On returning to the ship, I found that the barges had returned and that coaling was proceeding merrily.

From Marseilles to London nothing much occurred to remind us that half the earth was ablaze. Off Ushant a French warship sent a shot across our bows, but after one of her officers had interviewed our Captain we pursued our way peacefully enough and arrived in London without further incident. It was there that one was really drawn into the vortex, so to speak. But my stay in England was not fated to be a long one. I was offered a commission in either the Dublin Fusiliers or Leinsters, but when I was about to accept this I received a cable ordering me to return to Egypt at once. It was not the kind of order one can argue about and I went.

Luckily it was not a civilian job that awaited my arrival. Apparently General Sir John Maxwell, who was then GOC in Egypt, had applied to the Director-General Egyptian Survey Department for someone to act as Map Officer, and I had been recommended. Therefore I soon found myself temporary and local (the 'local' part disappeared later) captain attached to General Staff Intelligence, of which Colonel G. Clayton was at that time chief. The work that I had to do at first was not exactly exciting. It was to organise an office from which all OCs could draw the maps they required. At times indeed I had to leave Cairo and interview various officers with regard to their cartographical wants. Then I always felt like a commercial traveller. But I found that I had to tell many of my 'clients' – even generals – what they did want.

About this time I heard rather an amusing story, though I cannot vouch for the truth of it. One night at some dinner a lady asked Sir John Maxwell how many troops he had on the Canal. 'I don't really know,' replied the General, 'but I do know that if I am sent any more I shall have to lengthen the Canal.'

The organisation of a map office was not a very long job, and once it was done I found myself employed as an Intelligence Officer pure and simple. In this billet life was not without its excitements. I remember that one of the final missions that I was sent on was to take some very confidential papers to Port Said and to deliver them personally to the Captain of HMS *Swiftsure*. But when I had knocked up that officer at about midnight it was only to be informed that my papers were for HMS *Doris*, which had just sailed for the Syrian coast. The only way to reach her was to set off in pursuit in a torpedo-boat, and this I promptly did. I should think that torpedo-boat belonged to the oldest class in the Navy, and directly we were clear of the harbour her captain, a warrant officer, asked me if I knew anything about the coast. I answered that I did – from the land. 'Well,' he said, 'that's more than I do. I'm a gunner, I am, not a navigator.' He must have been a modest fellow though as we carried on all night and came up with the *Doris* while it was still dark. I was dressed in civilians and had to answer a good many questions before I was allowed to board her and do my job. But I handed over my despatches all right in the end, and returned in the TB to Port Said. All of us were very glad when we reached harbour again. We had put to sea at a moment's notice, and had no provisions on board barring cocoa, bread and margarine. The cocoa was A1.

But such jaunts as this were few and far between. Most of my time was spent either in the office or in the 'commercial travelling' I have already described. When engaged in the latter occupation

Ismailia was one of my most pleasant ports of call. There I was put up by Colonel Jennings Bramly, who was nominally Governor of Sinai, but had been forced to take up a strong position on the Canal as the Turks were in possession of his territory. Also at Ismailia there was the club, the memory of whose excellent cuisine haunts me still at times. Originally this club had been for the use of the Canal Company's pilots, but with the large influx of British troops it had become an international affair, and a perfect godsend to many a hungry khaki officer.

Office work and travelling! So the weeks passed, and I must admit that in spite of my military rank I felt anything but martial. But such a state of affairs was not to continue for long so far as I was concerned, and early in January, 1915, I was given the first hint of my future employment.

I had just returned to Cairo from Port Said, where I had been helping to make a report on the inundation which had been made by cutting through the banks of the Salt Company's canal and flooding a large depression in the desert – another little obstacle for Johnny Turk: about 130 square miles of nice clean water – when I was informed that I was Intelligence Officer, Liaison Officer and OC of a ship which had just been taken over by General Maxwell, and in which it was proposed to place two French seaplanes. The composite nature of the job made me catch my breath for a second, but as soon as I got the hang of it I was delighted at the prospect. I had always been keen on the sea. In fact when I was a boy I had only been prevented from trying for the Navy by my father's remarks that no Weldon had ever yet crossed the Irish Channel without being violently seasick. The idea of that weakness, however, no longer daunted me. I had long ago proved myself to be the exception to my family rule so that I was much pleased at the idea of a change of scene. But there should be moderation in all things, as I quickly realised when Colonel Newcombe, my direct chief, asked me if I thought that before I joined the ship I could get hold of a native boat, run down the north coast of Sinai, get into touch with the Arabs and carry out some propaganda work amongst them. That prospect did not please me, and I replied that I could easily get into touch with the Arabs, but the difficulty would be to get out of it again. I had mentioned that I had no wish to be shot or taken prisoner. My lack of enthusiasm saved me as it happened, but a few days later Captain White, who attempted to carry out this scheme, *did* get into touch with the Arabs and was taken prisoner, with the result that he spent the next four years in retirement somewhere in Asia Minor. The fates obviously intended me for a more restless existence.

2

The Aenne Rickmers

January–March, 1915

IT WAS ON THE 16th January, 1915, that I arrived at Port Said to take up my new job. The instructions I had received in Cairo had prepared me for something rather out of the ordinary, but it was not until I had talked matters over with Colonel Elgood, the Base Commandant, that I began to realise the complexity of the duties which I was expected to perform. I have already said that I was to be a kind of mixture of Liaison, Intelligence and Commanding Officer rolled into one, and that the seaplanes with which I was to work were French, but it soon appeared that this was not all. I was wanted to distribute spies, or more politely 'agents', behind the Turkish lines, and this little job also fell to my lot. At that time we knew that there were many people in Palestine and Syria who were willing to help us with information of enemy movements, etc., if we could arrange some system for collecting that news. The only way of doing this was to land agents on the coast behind Turkish positions, and to pick them up again when they had found out all our friends had to tell them. This landing and picking up was to be my share of the work, and I was to be lent a small naval steamboat, five Bluejackets and six Marines on purpose to do it.

As soon as I gathered exactly what I was in for, I realised that to land my agents at all I should need a boat fit for surf work, and boatmen who knew the coast to man it: so I spent most of my first day in Port Said hunting for recruits. Luckily they were not hard to find, for there happened to be four Syrian-Christian boatmen in the town who had been stranded there on the outbreak of war and were then at a loose end. These agreed to work with me at a price. So the next day I was able to join the ship.

The *Aenne Rickmers* was a German cargo-boat of about 7,000 tons, steel built and single screw. Formerly she was owned by the Rickmers family of Hamburg, but had been commandeered and was now attached to the French seaplane squadron. Her accommodation being much the same as is found on all cargo-boats of her size, a saloon to sit eight, a couple of two-berth cabins and a single bathroom. In the saloon was a portrait of 'Aenne', the daughter of Rickmers, and there it remained throughout all the cruises on board. In passing, I may mention that when I joined I was told that the ship had been borrowed for only six weeks. Little did I guess that she was to be my home for over two years.

The personnel was nearly as mixed as my job, and rather more cosmopolitan. The Captain, the chief engineer, the observers and the Bluejackets and Marines were English; the pilots and mechanics French; the mates and the crew Greek; one of the engineers was Maltese; and I myself, the OC, Irish. Moreover, the Captain was not then holding a companion, and the crew mostly belonged to a country – Greece – which had not come into the war. Also, we flew the Red Ensign: and the original cargo, worth about £250,000, was still on board. Yet two aeroplanes rested each on a hatch cover on the after well deck, and the uniformed sailors and mariners – lent by HMS *Swiftsure* – were obviously not men of peace. Taken all together, a regular Harry Tate shipload, reminiscent of the London Hippodrome at its best!

It was found out that our captain, Gaskell by name, was something of a character. Before the war he had been skipper of the *Milo*, a good steamer engaged on the Syrian coastal trade, and when I was introduced to him I mentioned that I had heard he was the best smuggler in those seas. I meant to pull his leg, but I think there must have been some truth in my remarks, because he took tremendous pains to explain that he could not have been anything of the sort.

In appearance he was enormous – well over six feet in height and weighing twenty-three stone. But in spite of his bulk he was very active, a wonderful swimmer – couldn't sink – and played a fine game of 'soccer' in goal. He should by rights have sat at the head of the table during meals, but as he could not fit into the chair, he sat on the settee which ran down one side of the table. He was the only one of us who could kick the beam in the ceiling of the saloon. Yet he had a high alto voice which sounded most comical from one of his bulk. Luckily he could speak Greek, otherwise the crew would never have understood him, and he had a thorough knowledge of the Eastern Mediterranean.

The only other Englishman amongst the ship's officers was Bishop, the chief engineer, a most capable man and a very pleasant companion, who had been in the Ports and Lights Department of the Egyptian Government and had volunteered for war service. We were together for nearly three years.

Before going on to relate any of my personal adventures I would like to say something about the French seaplane squadron with which I had become so suddenly connected. This squadron was commanded by Lieut. de Vaisseau de l'Escaille, one of the foremost French aviators, and had been sent to Egypt at the urgent request of General Maxwell. For some weeks the machines had been used flying from Port Said to reconnoitre the Sinai Peninsula, and their crews were symbolic of the Franco-British alliance, the pilots as a rule being French and the observers English.

Shortly before I arrived at Port Said one of these machines had been sent to the Gulf of Akaba on board the British cruiser *Minerva*. From there the plane, having as pilot a French quartermaster, Grall by name, and as observer Captain Stirling, late of the Dublin Fusiliers and Egyptian Army, was despatched on a flight inland, the idea being that it should reconnoitre Maan, a Turkish desert outpost. Owing to engine trouble, however, the machine made a forced landing at Wadi Arabi, some 29 miles from the sea. Both men were badly shaken, but having set fire to their 'bus', managed to crawl a good distance away and hide in the scrub. Of course it was impossible for them to remain where they were for long, but Grall was too weak to move far, so that it was agreed that Captain

Stirling should attempt to reach the shore alone, communicate with the ship, and bring back assistance. Delay meant certain disaster: and Stirling, leaving Grall his water bottle and chocolate, set off at once on his hazardous journey. Eventually, in a state of collapse, he reached the *Minerva* and gave the necessary information about the position of his companion. An armed party, 200 strong, landed and marched to the spot where he had left Grall, but no sign of the pilot could be found. After looking everywhere in the neighbourhood, the party returned reluctantly to the ship, which, after searching the coast, had to sail. A few hours later, however, the Captain said that he had a feeling that he ought to return. Luckily, he followed his intention and did so. It was night when the *Minerva* again arrived off the spot from which Stirling had been brought off, but the searchlight was turned on and it was not long before a figure of a man was observed on the shore. At once a boat was sent in, and Grall was rescued. It turned out later that when in hiding he had seen the search party in the distance and had mistaken them for Turks. So naturally he had lain doggo. But as soon as they had disappeared he had set off for the coast, which he reached at last after crawling painfully the whole 20 miles. A lucky escape!

Some of the French officers, who did not know the whole circumstances, were inclined to blame Stirling for what they called deserting Grall. This was most unjust. A more gallant officer than Frank Stirling does not exist, and as I knew both men personally I take this opportunity of stating exactly what happened. When I told Grall what was being said he was most indignant. In his opinion it was only Stirling's journey to the coast and the information he gave which saved him.

To return to the *Aenne*.

My period of comparative inaction at Port Said was not of long duration. I joined the ship as OC on the evening of 17th January, and at 1 a.m. the following day we sailed for the Syrian coast. The flying men with me on this my first trip were the two French pilots Lieut. de Vaisseau, Comte de Saizieu, and Quartermaster Grall, and two English observers, Captain J. R. Herbert and Captain Todd, late RAMC.

At noon on the 18th January we arrived off El Arish, which is about 30 miles from the border of Palestine, and is the only real town in Sinai. I had visited it in 1903 when employed on the survey of Northern Sinai. It is a clean town standing amidst sand-dunes about 10 miles from the sea and on the banks of the Wadi el Arish, the old river of Egypt. There was an old Turkish fort in the town which could easily be seen from the sea. It was now occupied by the enemy.

In the afternoon we hoisted out one of the 'planes with de Saizieu and Herbert for a flight to Kosseima. They returned safely after 2.5 hours. During their absence the second 'plane also carried out a successful reconnaissance along the coast, visiting El Arish, Rafa, Khan, Yunis and Gaza. Before the war no seaplane had been allowed ever to fly more than a mile away from the sea, and here we were doing flights of 90 miles overland.

The next day we lay off Gaza and sent a 'plane to Bir Saba (Beersheba of the Bible), which returned safely to the ship and reported considerable movement of the enemy troops on the Bir Saba–Hebron Road. From the first I made it a practice that immediately a 'plane returned to the ship the observer should write out a short report of what he had seen, which I then coded and sent out by wireless to GHQ Egypt. How I grew to hate coding as time went on! But reconnaissance was not our only business in that part of the world. We had brought an 'agent' with us from Port Said, and he had to be landed somewhere on the coast. So about midnight the *Aenne* stood in to about 3 miles from the shore, where she lay to while we launched the steamboat and our small native craft. Into the latter I tumbled the spy and two native boatmen, and deciding to be moderately comfortable for as long as possible, boarded the former. Then fixing up a tow-rope for the surf-boat, we headed for the shore.

The 'jumpy' part of the job began as soon as we reached the surf, when I had to transfer myself from the launch and trust myself to the boatmen to get me safely to the beach. There was a fair sea running, and the surf on the Palestine coast is never to be laughed at. Often it is impossible to run through it at all, and later on I had to often abandon the attempt. But the danger of capsizing was as nothing to the thought that, for all we could tell, we might reach the land only to find a Turkish patrol waiting for us. And once fairly in the surf there was no turning back. We simply had to go on and trust to luck. It was rather like taking a high dive without knowing whether there was water or a cement floor below. Even after I had got through the business successfully a few dozen times I never got over the uncomfortable feeling that I was heading straight for the hangman's rope or at best a Turkish prison and as we neared the shore that first time I could have sworn that I could see half the Turkish Army drawn up to meet us.

Actually, when we did bump the sand the beach was deserted, and all I had to do was to send off my man and row back to the steamboat, which I did with no unnecessary delay. I had no relish for hanging round a moment longer than I could help. The *Aenne* seemed to me about as near heaven as I cared for, for the time being, so turned round and headed for where we thought the *Aenne* was. After steaming a considerable time and not sighting her we began to get anxious. It was a pitch-dark night, and to make matters worse a big sea had got up and at every plunge the steamboat made we shipped water. I was sitting alongside the quartermaster, who was steering. He suddenly said in a hoarse whisper into my ear, 'It was a night like this when a steamboat same class as ours, sir, was lost off Sheerness with thirteen 'ands.' Comforting! We steamed on, but still no signs of the ship. At last we discovered that one of the Marines had been sitting with his sidearms-bayonet almost touching our compass. No wonder it was erratic!

The sea got so bad that at last I resorted to burning a flare in the hopes that the ship would see it. She did, and answered with three quick flashes of her masthead signal lamp. We reset our course, and after more severe buffeting at last reached her. Quite how glad I was when I saw her looming ahead out of the darkness it is impossible for me to say now. But 'very glad' is much too mild an expression.

The next day the 'planes were out again reconnoitring over El Arish and Lifan, and in the evening we headed for Gaza, where I intended to pick up the agent I had landed the previous night. I had arranged with him that he was to come down to the water's edge at 11 p.m. and show a light, and I had warned him to take care that his signal should only be visible from the sea. So when at about the given time we saw a light on the beach, I immediately repeated my performance of the night before and went ashore. But, once on the beach I found – nothing! For nearly an hour I stumbled about the neighbourhood, searching every nook and cranny: but all to no purpose. My man had disappeared. I was certain from his signal that he had been there, but he was there no longer: so at last, tired and disappointed, I returned to my boatmen and was rowed back through the surf. Some years afterwards I heard what had happened. My agent had been seen by some Turkish coastguards who had pounced on him while he was waiting for me on the beach, and shortly afterwards he had been hanged. The coastguards would only have had to wait another twenty minutes or so and *I* should have run straight into their arms. Why they did not guess what our man was up to when they found him with his light I have never been able to understand. But for their stupidity I am still sincerely thankful.

The next day (23rd January) we returned to Port Said. Not then knowing the fate of our agent, I had meant to send a 'plane over Gaza to show him we were still about if he could get down to the shore, but the glass was falling rapidly and a big sea was getting up so that it was impossible either to launch the machine or to go ashore through the surf. None of us enjoyed turning away from the job half-finished as it were but there was nothing else for it. As it happened, we should have gained nothing by waiting.

I have described in some detail this first cruise of mine in the *Aenne*, as it was fairly typical of many that followed. For the next six weeks we were working up and down the Syrian coast reconnoitring with our 'planes, landing and picking up agents, and generally making ourselves useful in the ways our superiors thought fit. As a rule our programme was to steam to a spot about five miles off shore and more or less opposite where the 'planes were to reconnoitre. Then we would lay to – and often actually drop our anchor, for there were no German submarines in the Mediterranean in those early days – and if the weather permitted hoist one or both machines over the side. This was always rather a ticklish job as the only winch we had to do it with was the ordinary one for hoisting cargo. A calm day was essential, and we had several mishaps through trying to get a 'plane away in a choppy sea, which was much worse than a big swell.

During one of our many cruises, I forget which, we hoisted out a seaplane one morning with de Saizieu as pilot and Herbert as observer for a flight over the Turkish lines. The 'plane rose well from the sea and commenced circling the ship so as to obtain a fair height before proceeding inland. Just as she was about 200 feet up, to our horror she suddenly seemed to stagger and then nosed-dived into the sea with an appalling crash. We at once sent away our steamboat to rescue the crew. On arriving at the wreck – she was smashed badly – we found Herbert and de Saizieu in the water hanging on to what was left of the machine. We quickly got them into the steamboat. The sea in the vicinity was covered with blown-out bladders, which had escaped out of the burst floats of the 'plane. One of these bladders Herbert had, very wisely, tied round his neck to assist him to float in case there was any delay in our getting to them. Neither of the men were hurt, although when they hit the water de Saizieu was held underwater, having got entangled in some wire stays. Herbert, on coming to the surface and not seeing him, dived and managed to free him. Poor de Saizieu was greatly depressed over losing his 'plane.

Fairly calm weather was also a necessity when it came to my night landing work. One can't run a small boat through the surf on the Syrian coast with anything like a real sea running. So we spent a large proportion of our time cruising about waiting for fair days, amusing ourselves as best we could by playing backgammon (for pennies) and having singsongs. The Frenchmen and our Bluejackets got on extremely well together, and never allowed the language difficulty to stand between them. They simply understood each other by instinct.

But we were seldom for any length of time without some grim reminder that war was tragedy. One such reminder I remember in particular. One morning towards the end of January, when we were lying off El Arish, we received a wireless telling us that a seaplane which had flown from Port Said in the direction of Bir-el-Abel (in Sinai) had not returned. I gave orders for the ship to cruise westwards keeping close inshore, for I hoped that the machine might have managed to reach the sea, and sure enough about midday we sighted a 'plane in the water. At first glance we thought that we could make out the figure of a man standing on the fusilage. But on closing in, we found that this was only the propeller blade and that the 'plane was derelict: so we launched a boat, towed the machine alongside the *Aenne* and hoisted it on board. The pilot's helmet and the observer's map and notes were still there. From the latter we gathered that they had left Port Said in the early afternoon of the day before and had flown to Kantara (on the Canal), where, owing to fog, they could see nothing, so had decided to return. The notes went on to state that owing to engine trouble they had come down in Bardawil Lake (Sinai), from which they rose to descend much in the same place a few minutes later. There the notes ended, so we concluded they must have risen again, had more engine trouble, landed in the sea near the beach, waded ashore, and that they must have either been captured or be even then walking to Port Said. Later we found out that the latter alternative was the right one. The pilot and observer had tried to reach Port Said on foot, and had almost reached their goal when they ran into one of our own posts, manned by Indian troops, and were fired at and were killed. No one was to blame as it was dark at the time, and it was only natural that coming from the direction they did, they should have been mistaken for the enemy. It was just bad luck. Patridge, late of the Ceylon contingent, was the observer, and the pilot was a French Bluejacket. Their bodies were brought in and buried in the Port Said cemetery.

Even at sea in those early days one was never quite safe from his own side. The *Aenne* had then no 'recognition number', and once we came precious near to being shelled by one of our own cruisers, HMS *Philomel*. She passed us at night and signalled asking who we were. As we were close inshore we did not think it wise to give our name, so hesitated before answering. Captain Russell of the *Philomel* told me some time afterwards that it was lucky we made up our minds when we did – another half-minute's silence and he would have put a shot into us! To quicken us up, I take it.

Shortly afterwards, not to be outdone by the *Philomel*, we challenged the *Rabenfels* (a sister ship of the *Aenne*, commandeered at the same time, and engaged in much the same kind of work). Somehow I don't think those on board were very much impressed when we asked for their number, and 'Have none: very pleased with your zeal' was the immediate reply.

3

Torpedoed

B Y THE BEGINNING of March, 1915, all of us on board the *Aenne* were heartily sick of the Palestine coast. Probably one's idea of monotony is not the same in wartime as it is in the piping days of peace, and certainly at that time we found our work monotonous. I remember I was accused of being the only person who got any 'fun' on account of my occasional night stunts. Personally I think a fellow who flew 60 miles inland in one of our not very new Nieuports ought to have got all the 'fun' he wanted. But opinions differ. Anyhow, there was soon to be plenty of 'fun' for all of us – more of it than we had any use for.

On the morning of the 4th March we were cruising quietly off Gaza when we received a wireless from Port Said asking how much coal we had on board. We replied at once, stating the amount – 460 tons – and wondered why on earth the information was wanted. We had not to wait long for an answer. The next thing we knew was that we were ordered, by wireless, to proceed as quickly as possible to – then followed a longitude and latitude. Wild excitement reigned while the captain looked up his charts. The given position turned out to be the Gulf of Smyrna.

Of course we were all delighted, and I patted myself on the back for having insisted on coaling when last in port. But when I say 'we' were delighted I mean only the British and French elements on board. The Greek crew did not look on things in the same light, and as soon as they knew what was in the wind 'got the breeze up' properly. So much so in fact that I had to post sentries over the 'planes for fear the Greeks would try to damage them in the hope that we should have to return to Port Said.

Well, away we headed for Smyrna. I had wirelessed to ask permission to call at Limassol, in Cyprus, to re-provision, but received a reply not to do this unless absolutely necessary, as we could provision from the ships we were going to meet. I had on board as pilots Destrem and Grall, the observers being Todd, Sir R. Paul and Williams: the latter had just joined us, and originally came from the Ceylon Rifles. We had been doing just over 10 knots, but owing to a heavy sea and head wind were soon reduced to 7. At noon on the 5th we passed the Island of Rhodes, a fine- looking country. Destrem told me that it was here the *Bisson* was blown up. The French always have a ship of this name in the Navy, called after a Lieut. Bisson, a French naval officer who during the war of England and France v. Turkey and Egypt about the time of the battle of Navarino, being in command of a small ship (a prize) when it was overhauled by a Turkish man-o'-war, blew up both his ship and himself in order to avoid capture, only one petty officer being saved. A splendid acknowledgement of a fine deed.

At about 10 a.m. on the 6th we arrived off the Gulf of Smyrna, and received a wireless from the *Swiftsure* slightly altering our rendezvous, and telling us to steam in towards Smyrna town which is at the head of the gulf. This we proceeded to do at about 12.30 p.m., and shortly afterwards we sighted a five-funnel cruiser, the Russian ship *Askold* – commonly known as the 'packet of Woodbines' – which came tearing up and challenged us. Our reply being satisfactory – we had a recognition number then – we steamed on into the gulf and came up with the *Triumph*, *Swiftsure* and *Euryalus* in line ahead with five trawlers (North Sea) sweeping in advance of them. The battleships were all at it, busily shelling the forts on shore. Naturally we were very much pleased and excited we were in the middle of a real 'naval fight', even though it were only ships versus forts. The Captain asked me what I thought he should do, and suggested anchoring some distance away from the ships in action. But as our original orders were to join the ships, I said that we ought to follow them, especially as we were all keen to see as much as we could. So the fat old *Aenne Rickmers* fell into line and waddled after the last ship. I am afraid that we were 'not much addition', as they say in Ireland, to the bombardment, for our armament only consisted of one Maxim gun and about a dozen service rifles (long, not short) and bayonets.

Shortly afterwards the leading ship (the *Euryalus*, with Admiral Sir R. Pierce on board) turned – all of us following – and came out to Vourlah (the quarantine station for Smyrna), where we all anchored for the night. I received a signal from the flagship ordering me to go on board the flagship *Euryalus* to see the Admiral. This I did, taking with me our captain and Captain Destrem. The Admiral had us down in his cabin and explained that in the morning the ships were going to steam into Smyrna and bombard the forts. He wanted us to come on board his flagship during the bombardment, and then to return to the *Aenne Rickmers* and hoist out a 'plane to fly in over the forts and see what damage the fire from the ships had done. When this had been agreed to we returned to the *Aenne*. That evening some wounded Bluejackets in charge of a Surgeon Patterson of the *Triumph* were brought on board as it was thought that it would be quieter for them with us than if they stopped in their own ship, which was going to take part in the bombardment.

At 8.30 a.m. the next day our observers, pilots and I went on board the *Euryalus*. After morning prayers on the quarterdeck every man took up his battle-quarters, all watertight compartments were closed, the anchor weighed, and, in line ahead with the *Euryalus* leading, we steamed in towards the forts.

Commander Marriott took charge of our little party and asked us where we thought we should like to be stationed, and suggested one of the fighting tops: but Todd, one of our observers, said that he would get giddy climbing up. Marriott looked surprised, and said that he understood that an observer who went up in an aeroplane should be used to heights: but it was a curious fact that Todd, although he never felt giddy in an aeroplane, no matter at what height it was, always got giddy climbing a ladder. When we had to board a ship I always had to follow him closely up the Jacob's ladder in case he fell, and he was one of our best observers. So in the end we decided for the bridge, and there we went.

For some time the battleships did not open fire, and the position of the forts was pointed out to us by Captain Burmester and Major O'Sullivan, a Marine. The latter I had met years before when he was in the Egyptian Army in the Soudan. Then, having seen all we wanted to, we were put on board one of the trawlers and taken back to the *Aenne*. The skipper of this trawler was a bit of a character. He was a typical North Sea fisherman, over sixty years old, and a fine specimen of a man. There he was in his little wheel-house dressed in exactly the same kit as he wore in the North Sea – two jerseys, muffler and seaboots. He explained to me that he always had to have a thin man at the wheel as otherwise two couldn't have fitted into the wheel-house. He was a fine old boy with a wife and eleven children at Grimsby, but 'doing his bit.' I asked him how he liked it, and he replied, 'It's orl right, sir, but I would like to be able to 'it back.' In those days the trawlers were not armed.

After a while the ships began to bombard the forts, which replied, and things got lively. The *Triumph*, I remember, got a shell through her funnel. When darkness came on two enemy searchlights began to play on the stretch of water outside Smyrna harbour, which had been mined, in the hope of spotting our trawlers sweeping. The minute a searchlight appeared, bang would go a 6-incher at it from either the *Swiftsure* or the *Triumph*. It was most amusing to watch, rather like a man in a barrel at a fair when he puts his head out and you have cockshots at him with balls, and he ducks his head inside the barrel to avoid them. When the ships fired, out would go the lights. I don't think we hit any of them.

On the 8th we again anchored off Vourlah and the ships continued to bombard the forts. The Russian cruiser *Askold* came in and fired several rounds at the quarantine station. When asked why she did that, she replied she had been fired at from there. No one believed her. She had a bad reputation of making targets of inoffensive villages, etc.

That evening the Commodore of the Sweepers – which were known to our men as the 'Kippers' – came on board the *Aenne* to tea. He hailed from Grimsby, and, as he was a married man and was going in to sweep the minefield that night, he brought with him his Will, which I witnessed, and which he left with us for safe keeping. After dark the ships opened heavy fire on the searchlights to keep them down while the 'Kippers' were sweeping.

Early next morning, 9th March, we received a signal to say that Trawler No. 285 had blown up on a mine during the night while sweeping and that twelve of the crew were missing – five survivors. At 10.30 a.m. a general signal was made from the flagship to say that a Memorial Service would be held on board her. The French pilot, Lieut. Destrem, and I set off to attend. The sea was very rough, and we were wet through by the time we arrived on board. The service, which was most impressive, was held on the quarterdeck, the five survivors attending. I was delighted to see my old friend the skipper and father of eleven amongst them. Apparently the '285' bumped a mine and, as the skipper told me, simply fell to pieces. He himself was in the water for an hour and a half before being picked up by a launch.

In the afternoon we hoisted out a 'plane with Destrem and Paul in it, which flew in towards Smyrna Harbour. They were fired at by the batteries with shrapnel, but returned safely and reported that the Turks had blocked the mouth of the harbour by sinking two ships across it – most likely Allied ships that were in the port when war was declared. So off I went to the flagship to report the result of the flight. On the way I saw a small sailing boat coming out from the shore, and ran down to her. When I got close, her sail was furled and a man stood up in the bows vigorously waving a white pair of drawers, I presumed as a white flag. I ran alongside, keeping my rifle handy, and found she was manned by four Turkish sailors and had two passengers on board. One of these, who was dressed in a black tail-coat, stood up and told me that he was the American Consul-General from Smyrna (there was no doubt about the American part of him, to judge by the accent) and that his companion was the secretary of the Vali (i.e. Governor) of Smyrna, and that they wished to speak to the Admiral. Having carefully examined the boat to see that there were no bombs or such things on board, I took the passengers into my launch and, towing their boat, went alongside the flagship. Then, having handed the Captain my report, I returned to the *Aenne*, and a little later saw the American Consul and his crowd being towed towards the shore.

I should have mentioned before this that every night all the ships were darkened and all lead-lights lowered so as not to present a target for the enemy's guns. That evening a general signal was made, saying a truce had been arranged till 10 a.m. on Thursday, it then being Tuesday evening. This was welcome news, as it meant we could show our lights at night and not worry about deadlights, etc. As a matter of fact *our* deadlights were manufactured by pasting thick brown paper over the port- holes and shading them as best we could with curtains or canvas. All the ships had been ordered to fly a white flag on the foremast, and, not having prepared for war as the Germans did (refer to German officer captured on the Canal with a white flag on him), we had to resort to hoisting our cleanest tablecloth.

That night we retired to bed at about 11 p.m. at peace with – hardly the world, but anyway our local enemies. (I should mention that my cabin was situated on the bridge just over the Captain's.) Suddenly, at 2.05 a.m. (11th March) – I knew the exact time as my watch stopped then – after I had been quietly sleeping for some hours I was pitched out of my bunk, hit the ceiling and fell on the floor of the cabin. I naturally felt rather confused, and remember saying to myself, 'There you are again at your old tricks – walking in your sleep,' and proceeded to get back into my bunk. Then I realised, however, that I had heard a loud explosion and also heard frightened yells and screaming, so I promptly got into my trousers and coat – it was bitterly cold weather – and stepped out on to the bridge. There I naturally expected to find the officer of the watch and the look-out man, but not a sign of anyone was to be seen.

While I was trying to think what had happened I heard a 'ping' go by my head followed by the bang of a rifle. Startled, I looked down on the bridge-deck and saw a funny sight. There was the stout Captain with nothing on except a short nightdress (he never wore pyjamas) calling out at the top of his voice, 'We're sinking! We're sinking! Get the boats out!' As a matter of fact he was a bit late as our gallant Greek crew, headed by their Greek officers, had already done so. I saw one lifeboat that would have held forty men rowing away from the ship with three of the crew and the chief officer (Greeks) on board. That put an end to my confusion, and I ran down to the main deck, where I came to the conclusion that we had either been torpedoed or had been bumped by a mine.

It was pitch dark. The ship was awash with water and very much down by the head – and going down further. I found all the crew and officers had bolted with the exception of the Captain, Bishop, the chief engineer and a Maltese engineer whom Bishop had caught just as he was scrambling into a boat and had put back – forcibly – into the engine-room. I may mention that this Maltese wrote to me a couple of years later and asked what reward he was going to get for his bravery on this occasion. Todd, Paul and Williams, the observers, and Lieut. Destrem and Surgeon Patterson were naturally still on board, as were also my Marines and Bluejackets, who fell in on deck and waited for orders.

Our first thoughts were for the wounded men who were in the 'tween-decks. I went down to see them and told them we wouldn't desert them. I remarked to one – the cook of the *Euryalus* who couldn't move, having been wounded in the legs – that it was a bit of a shock. 'Yes, sir,' he replied, 'what one might call a rude awakening.' They were all quite calm. Then I went back to the bridge and found there the signal-boy, Sloman by name, dressed in nothing except a vest and a pair of drawers. I gave him some clothes out of my cabin and told him to signal with my Orilux lamp to the other ships that we had been mined or torpedoed and that our crew had bolted with all the boats. The reply came quickly, 'Are you in danger of sinking?' It looked very like it, so I answered, 'Probably,' and asked for a boat to take off the wounded men. The Captain had given me permission to take charge and signal as he was getting the winch ready to hoist out the wounded. There was no one else on board who understood the infernal thing.

Meanwhile Bishop and Paul were down in the holds trying to find out what water we were making and what was our chance of keeping afloat, while Todd, Patterson and Williams were getting the wounded ready to leave the ship.

It was not long before a picquet boat ran alongside and we got all the wounded away in her. I gave my friend the cook all my codes and our letter-box, with orders only to deliver them into the hands of the Captain of whatever ship he was taken to, which, as I heard afterwards, he faithfully did. Then one more boat came alongside, and as it was no good keeping anybody, I ordered all the Marines, Bluejackets and young Williams to go away in her. The PO of the Bluejackets refused to take his men away and leave us till I told him it was an order, then he saluted and went down into the boat with his men.

There were now seven of us on board, including Sloman the signaller and Trett the wireless operator. We all stood about on the deck with our ankles in water wondering when the final plunge was coming, till I suggested that it would be drier – anyway for the time – if we adjourned to the saloon. Meanwhile the men-o'-war had slipped their cables and proceeded to sea, leaving us to our fate. Of course they were only doing the right thing as at any moment they might have been torpedoed also.

Naturally we were rather excited and all complained of exceedingly dry mouths. Someone suggested that a drink would not be amiss, but the steward had bolted with the keys. Luckily I remembered that I had one bottle of Irish whiskey in my cabin. It was the only Irish whiskey on board, and I had been keeping it for St Patrick's Day, the 17th March. I debated in my mind, however, and came to the conclusion that we had better have it out at once as perhaps we should not be alive on the 17th, so out it came.

Whilst we were drinking I happened to glance at the door and to my surprise saw a Marine standing outside. It was my corporal, Shrimpton by name. I asked what he was doing there, and why he had not obeyed my order and gone away in the last boat. Thereupon he merely saluted and said, 'The Marines never desert their officers, sir,' so although annoyed, I promptly forgave him and brought him out a whiskey. The time passed very slowly. After an hour or so I went out and had a look round, and came to the pleasing conclusion that, although the ship was very much down by the head, she was now stationary. Bishop, who had examined the damage pretty thoroughly, reported that she had been hit on the starboard side in No. 1 hold, but that the bulkhead between No. 1 and No. 2 was all right and that as long as it held he thought that we should keep afloat. It was then that we thanked our stars that we had all the original cargo on board. No. 1 hold, where we had been struck, was full of great baulks of timber – white oak – while No. 2 contained antimony ore which made a splendid buttress for the bulkhead. Certainly that cargo was worth all of a quarter of a million to us.

None of us slept that night. When daylight came there we were still floating at anchor, very much down by the head and awash, and not a ship in sight. Still, the sight of the cutter which the *Euryalus* had left to stand by us cheered us up a little and reminded us that we were not forgotten. We had the sub-lieutenant in charge on board, gave him a drink, and made him write his name in our visitors' book. By that time we had decided that with any luck we should not sink.

But we were to have another few minutes of excitement, for while it was still early the signal-boy came to me and reported that an enemy's ship was coming out of Smyrna Harbour probably, as he said, 'to finish us off'.

We watched her anxiously, but when she got to the harbour mouth she turned broadside on to us and then gradually began to sink. We felt relieved. The Turks were merely completing the blocking of the harbour. (I heard afterwards that this block ship was the Ellerman boat the *City of Chios*.)

About 10 a.m. – morning of the 11th – the look-out reported that the fleet was in sight on its way back, and we knew that the worst of our troubles were over. Shortly afterward, I was on board the flagship making my report. The officers were all very kind and pleased to see us. They told me that they had never expected to find the *Aenne* still afloat. They had picked up all our deserting crew before they left, but had had to let the boats drift away. I heard that when our Greeks rowed alongside the *Euryalus* in the dark, imploring to be saved, Commander Marriott asked them where the wounded Bluejackets were, and when they told him that they were still in the ship he knocked the first officer down, as the man richly deserved.

While I was on board the *Euryalus* the Turkish Governor and another Turkish officer, Nazem Bey, came on board to see the Admiral, and I was told that I could not see him then as he was busy making up his mind whether or not he would hang the two Turks. They had attacked us while flying the white flag. In justice to them I ought to mention here that it was a small TB that did us in. She had been lying outside, concealed amongst the islands, and not knowing of the truce, came in and let fly at us. The boat carried only three torpedoes, and probably missed with the first two shots. She evidently went for the *Aenne Rickmers* under the impression that she was an ammunition ship, and that if she blew up the explosion would damage the other ships lying close by. One of the Turks asked me if I had been in the torpedoed ship. I replied, 'Yes, thank you,' and he congratulated me on my escape. He appeared to be a decent sort.

A little later I returned to the *Aenne* and a work party came on board to see what they could do. Everybody was busy picking up the bits of torpedo that were lying about the decks. I found some pieces actually in my cabin on the bridge. They must have been blown through the partially closed door.

After much labour the working party got a collision mat over the hole in our side. Then our Greek crew were sent back to us and we were told to sail for Lemnos, convoyed by the *Swiftsure*. So, before parting with the ships, I sent all our party on board the *Swiftsure* for safety's sake, but Lieut. Destrem absolutely refused to leave his seaplanes or me, though he sent away his mechanics. When the Greek crew were coming up the side, what should I see but the ship's baker dressed in my overcoat! He had seized it out of the saloon when he bolted. I promptly had a few words with him about the matter. Our escort went right ahead and we toiled after her, burying our nose in the sea. Besides putting the collision mat over the hole – and, by the way, it was sucked in just after we started – the working party had shored up the bulkhead between No. 1 and No. 2 holds. All the same, we had a most trying night as soon as we got out of the Gulf of Smyrna and headed north. There was a strong head wind and a heavy sea. It was bitterly cold, and we were all worn-out. For some hours Lieut. Destrem very kindly relieved the Captain on the bridge. Although we had our Greek officers back we did not let them take a watch or have anything to do with the navigating of the ship. At one time during the night the Captain came to me in my cabin and said that he did not think we could keep afloat much longer. I went out on the bridge and found he had set the crew to make rafts out of the hatch covers. But it was so bitterly cold that I told him that I preferred going down with my blankets round me rather than prolonging the agony by clinging on to a hatch cover in an icy sea. So back I went to bed, though not to sleep. Every few minutes I could hear the Captain singing out to his men watching the shored-up bulkhead, 'Is that bulkhead giving?' Cheery what? When I got up at daybreak I found that we were certainly in a pretty bad way, for not only was the *Aenne* down by the head, but she had developed a heavy list also.

Still, we struggled on. Every hour was bringing us nearer to safety. Moreover, that our safety was looked upon as assured by the powers that be was quickly proved, for while we were still butting our way towards Lemnos I received a signal to say 'Intelligence Officer' – that was me – 'is ordered by GOC Egypt to return to Port Said as soon as possible. I' – that was the Admiral – 'shall not require seaplanes again.' When this message reached me I was wondering if I should ever put my foot on any shore again – let alone Port Said.

That message seemed a little ironical at the time, but the crowning jest was still to come. Come it did. When at last we arrived at Mudros, weary but triumphant, we were flying the Blue Ensign – why, goodness only knows – and no sooner had we waddled into harbour and dropped anchor, feeling the real thing in warworn heroes, than we received a signal to lower the Blue Ensign of ours at once and fly the Red one instead. So that was all the welcome we got after all our adventures. A pretty snub!

4

At Mudros

March–April, 1915

IT WAS IN THE afternoon of 12th March that we butted our way into Mudros Harbour, and already the Dardanelles adventure was in the air. The great land-locked bay was packed with battleships, transports and colliers. On the island itself camps of British and colonial troops were springing up everywhere, and although, as I soon found out, no one seemed to know exactly what was toward, everybody knew that such concentration was not meaningless. The 'holiday' could not last for long, and officers and men were all trying their hardest to make the best of it.

But the first thought of all of us on the *Aenne* was provisions. We had practically run out, so informal foraging parties were the rule for the next few days. We drew the store ship *Swanly* blank, and all we could find in the picturesque but very dirty little town of Mudros was unlimited supplies of fish and macaroni. Luckily Bishop ran into a friend on board the *Favourette* and brought back something more solid, whilst Destrem raided the French cruisers and managed to obtain some of that excellent wine the French issue as a ration. In the meantime Captain Lefroy and Commander Kitson of the *Swiftsure* brought a large working party on board and started in to get out the cargo in order to lighten the ship so that they could make a proper examination of the damage. At the same time Mudros was a great meeting place of friends and acquaintances from all over the world. I was always running into people I had met at home and in Egypt, so as there was nothing much for me to do on board the *Aenne*, I spent a good deal of my time paying calls. I received calls also, and sometimes more than I wanted, for it was not long before whole boatloads of soldiers from various transports began to find our 'hole' an irresistible attraction. The men were always pulling across the harbour to have a look at 'the ship which had been torpedoed'. There must have been thousands of them altogether, and as the cargo was shifted and the ship rode higher out of the water the hole showed up really well. It measured 12 feet by 26, and the iron framework of the hold was bent and twisted into every conceivable shape.

Of course the men who merely looked at the damage from their boats were no trouble to us at all, but one day a large party of Irish-Australians pulled alongside us and their officers asked permission for them to come on board. At first they all rushed off to No. 1 hold to inspect the famous hole. That was all right, but when they streamed aft to look at the 'planes I had to ask their officers to keep them from touching these machines. But Australian discipline was not that of the British, and the men paid no attention to orders and kept on poking their fingers against the fabric of the wings to see what it was made of. Seeing that they took no attention of their combatant officers, I asked their padre to tackle them. He did, and at once the difference was apparent. 'All right, Father,' they said, and immediately stood back.

Talking of the Australians, it was in Mudros that I met the one man who seemed privileged to tell them what he thought of them. One day I was in the shop of a Greek barber waiting my turn for a 'hair-cut'. A good many Australians were also waiting, and one, a very small man with a wizened-up face, was holding forth to his companions.

He looked about forty-five and had about six different war ribbons on his chest.

'You Australians,' I heard him say (he himself was wearing the Australian uniform), 'are first class' – he paused and his listeners looked pleased: then his eyes twinkled – 'at swearing and drinking,' he finished emphatically.

The men round him took it well and laughed heartily. Apparently he was a bit of a character and no one took offence at what he said.

Funnily enough, when I asked him a few questions out of curiosity I found that he had once been in the Sherwood Foresters and had then been my cousin's groom. When I mentioned my cousin's name he grew quite enthusiastic. In fact, 'What, old Frankie!' he burst out. 'Why, I and he won (or nearly won) the Viceroy's Cup. Good old Frankie!' I wished Major Frank Weldon, DSO, had been there to hear him.

To return to the *Aenne*. One day we received the news that Grall, the French flying pilot, had been awarded the Medaille Militaire. We were all delighted. No man deserved it more. We all, officers and men, both French and British, donned our best uniforms and fell in on deck, and Destrem, after a short speech in French, pinned the medal on Grall. I made a short (very) speech also in French (bad), and then called for three cheers for Grall.

We had decided that we would celebrate St Patrick's Day with something in the nature of a feast, so in the morning Paul, Destrem and Williams (our flying men who had returned on board) went ashore as a foraging party. They could find nothing worthy of the occasion in Mudros itself, so they set out inland to search the villages. At first they drew a blank, but at last they arrived at one where there was a flock of sheep. Immediately Paul, the linguist of the party, set to to trade. First he tried French, then Italian, then Arabic, and afterwards what he called Greek, but all with no result. Even signs worked no better, and he was just about to give up in despair when one of the villagers suddenly said to him in English, with a first-class American accent, 'Say, what is it you really want?' Paul took the snub, but bought sheep. It appeared that many of the villagers had been to America, made a little money, returned to their native land and bought patches of land.

It was the morning after this that I went on board Admiral Sir Rosslyn Wemyss's yacht *Imogene* to ask him if there was any hope of our ship being repaired as she was urgently needed by Sir John Maxwell for work off the Syrian coast. The Admiral was charming, and told me he was expecting a salvage ship from Malta, which could take the *Aenne* in hand as soon as it arrived. Later I saw more of Admiral Wemyss. He struck me as not only being a gentleman in the best sense of the word but also as being extremely businesslike and capable.

Afterwards I saw him at Gallipoli when he was in charge of the 'covering ships', and then he appeared even to an outsider like myself to be the right man in the right place. He was loved by his men, from the senior officer down to the youngest boy, and he was always cool, cheerful and sympathetic. I remember that he had the greatest admiration for the RNR men, who formed a large proportion of his crew, and I overheard him remark to his Flag-Commander that he did not know what he should have done without them.

The next few days passed without any incident but a bad blow – and it could blow in Mudros! One night our launch broke loose and we had to chase her in the dark. Boats were adrift everywhere in the harbour, and our launch, when captured, had a busy time bringing them alongside. More than one boat's crew we had to put up for the night. In the midst of the gale our captain thought it wise to drop another anchor, whereupon, hearing the noise, our gallant Greek crew rushed up on deck crying that we had been torpedoed. Thank goodness we paid them off a few days later.

Except for the concentration of troops, very little happened during our stay at Mudros to remind us of active warfare. Once a German 'plane flew high over the island, but was far away before the machine we sent up after it could get within fighting distance. Perhaps our minds were jogged most sharply one morning towards the end of the month when the battleship *Inflexible* arrived in harbour with a bad list. She had struck a mine near Gallipoli, and had only been kept afloat by the closing of the watertight doors. We learnt afterwards that sixty poor fellows had been trapped in a torpedo flat and drowned.

Incidentally the damage done to the *Inflexible* ended our chances of getting the *Aenne* repaired for some time. Naturally the former was much more important than our ship, and the men who had been working at our hole had been ordered to leave and get on with the repairs of the battleship. This meant that to leave the 'planes we had on board where they were was a mere waste of materiel, so I was not surprised to get orders to transfer them to our old friend the *Rabenfels*, which had arrived in harbour a day or two before. Unfortunately, the Captain and Bishop had gone off to Mudros in the launch and had forgotten to send it back to us, so that as there was a strong wind blowing it was impossible for us to tow the machines across. Eventually a line was brought over from the *Rabenfels* to which we made fast the 'planes, when they were hauled over by the winch to their new home. This took time, and de l'Escaille, who was in charge, wanted to sail in a hurry. Naturally he was angry, and when our captain came back in the launch just as the job was finished there was a bit of a scene. Even when the enraged de l'Escaille was being rowed away he stood up in the boat and, pointing at our skipper, kept on calling out, 'You are a very bad captain. You are a very bad captain.'

But the transfer of the 'planes was only the beginning of a steady withdrawal of men and materiel. On Easter Eve, 3rd April, we were told that the flagship required the use of our launch. This meant that those few of us who were still on board had no means of getting about except by pulling ourselves in a row-boat, and by that time there were very few of us left to pull. The flying men, of course, had gone with their 'planes, and the crew had been paid off, so on Easter Day our great 7,000-ton boat was inhabited by exactly five men – the Captain, the chief engineer, the cook, the steward and myself. Without the launch it was too much like playing Swiss Family Robinson to suit my tastes.

Furthermore, few as we were, we had our troubles. After Easter the weather got worse and worse, and for three days it blew a whole gale.

On the morning of the 6th April, just before I turned out, I felt the ship give a couple of irregular shivers or jerks. I ran out on deck and found both cables had parted. Since our cargo had been removed from No. 1 hold the fore part of the ship was naturally very light and stood high out of the water, and so was very exposed. Of course we had no steam up. All we could do was to hoist a signal 'not under control', and then we stood and waited to see what our fate was to be. There we were, a great, heavy ship drifting about a harbour packed with men-o'-war, transports, storeships and tankers (i.e. oil ships), wondering which we were going to collide with and damage. Soon our signal was spotted, frantic sirens sounded, and we received all sorts of advice; 'Let your anchor go,' etc. We only missed ramming two ships by inches, and eventually ran ashore in a little bay, where we remained hard and fast.

Immediately afterwards we received a signal from the flagship to say we were to remain where we were. This order was easy enough to obey as, with the best will in the world, five of us could hardly have pushed the *Aenne* from the shore. Later in the morning we did manage to get a hawser ashore and tie her up properly. Next morning we got out our spare anchor, fixed it up ashore, and made fast to it with another hawser.

Admiral Sir Rosslyn Wemyss came on board and started to congratulate the Captain on having beached the ship, after the cable parted, on the only sandy beach in the harbour, when foolishly he blurted out that we had no steam up and had drifted there by luck. If he had kept his mouth shut he would have been in a fair way to much *Kudos*. The Admiral then inspected our 'hole'. He was most affable, and said that he was afraid that I was having a hard and dull time, and suggested lending me to the Australians. If he had I might still have had a hard but certainly not a dull time. I respectfully pointed out to him, however, that General Maxwell, C-in-C Egypt, expected me to keep an eye on the cargo, for which he had given a guarantee: and I thought that I had better stay on the *Aenne*, even if the job was one which I was sure W. W. Jacobs night watchman would have done far better than I would.

As a matter of fact it was just as well I did stay on board as every naval commander in the harbour who wanted wood seemed to look on us as fair game. The usual procedure was to send over a steam launch in charge of a 'Snotty', who would come on board and calmly announce, 'I have been sent to get some planks.' My counter measures with such visitors were simple. I used to usher him into the saloon, get him to write his name in the visitors' book, stand him a drink and express my regret that he could not have what he wanted. If the ship had been left with no one in charge she would have been like a dead camel in the desert when the vultures have finished with it.

About this time things were very dull on board. The Captain left us to take command of a tug, and Bishop and I were left to amuse ourselves as best we could. We soon got bored with watching the transports which kept on pouring in from the south, and, as we were very short of comforts, we used to go ashore after crabs. In one place especially we caught some fine ones, which we duly appreciated until we discovered a dead horse – a very dead horse – just near their feeding ground. After that we rather lost interest in crabs.

By this time we had learnt that a landing on Gallipoli was to be attempted, but although we were naturally deeply interested, we were beginning to think that we personally should be at Mudros for ever. For the Admiral informed me unofficially that he could do nothing at present towards repairing the 'hole'. So we settled down to a period of monotonous waiting. Even in the one enterprise we did undertake we were not successful, perhaps luckily for us, as things turned out. We had spotted a derelict motor launch which had gone ashore, and Bishop, having looked her over, decided that he could tinker her up all right. So we decided to 'pinch' her, and set out in the dinghy to do so. But just as we were slowly making towards her we saw a naval picquet boat steaming in. We slowed down and waited. The picquet boat made straight for the launch, took her in tow, turned and headed for the flagship. Our launch was the Admiral's private one. No wonder we were left cold.

By the middle of April there was no mistaking the signs that the big adventure would not be long delayed. At that time I ran into various old friends belonging to the 29th Division, and I was fairly often a guest on the transports which carried them. One of these, the *Ausonia*, was tied up alongside the now famous *River Clyde* and I saw the working parties cutting the rectangular openings in her sides through which the gangways were to be lowered. On the morning of the 17th April I watched the Dublins and Munsters filing into her. I remember one man called to a pal, 'Come on, Mike: come into yer coffin,' a jest which was to come very nearly true for many of them. I was so bored sitting doing nothing on the old *Aenne* that I asked Colonel Rooth, who commanded the Dublins, if I might go with him. At first he said 'yes', but afterwards refused on account of the questions which might be asked later. It was lucky for me that he had that afterthought.

That afternoon I was told that the Turkish TB that had got us had attacked the transport *Manitu* somewhere off Chios.

The captain of the TB behaved most leniently. He hailed the transport, said that he was going to sink her, and gave the captain five minutes in which to abandon the ship. The captain of the *Manitu* replied that he couldn't do it in the time. The captain of the TB then gave ten minutes. There was evidently a bit of a rush on board, and many of the men threw themselves into the sea or were upset out of the boats as these were being hurriedly lowered. The TB fired three torpedoes at the transport and missed her; probably she was too close and they went under her. Then, evidently having no more torpedoes, the TB cleared off, and the transport picked up as many of the men who were still floating as she could and came on to Mudros. We were told fifty-four men were drowned. It was a bad show. The *Manitu* had field-guns on deck for the purpose of defending herself against attack, but it was reported that all the ammunition for the guns was somewhere in the bottom of the hold and inaccessible.

The next day I rowed over to the *Imogene* to see the Admiral. As I have said, we only had a dinghy to get about in, so I pulled stroke and the Greek cook bow. When I got alongside the ship I put on my tunic, went on board and did my job. On returning on deck I found a 'Snotty' at the top of the gangway, who saluted and politely asked me if he could call my boat for me. I said 'yes', of course. Then, looking round, he told me my boat wasn't there. So I pointed to the dinghy with our greasy old cook in it. The 'Snotty's' face was a picture as he watched me take off my tunic and pull away. He naturally thought I had come in some naval boat. This 'Snotty's' name was Drewry, and later on he won the VC at Gallipoli.

5

The Gallipoli Landing

April, 1915

B Y THIS TIME I had quite made up my mind that I should be
stuck at Mudros for at least another month or so: but I was
soon undeceived, for on the afternoon of 18th April Commander
Marriott sent me a note that I was to report on board the *Euryalus*
at 5 p.m. the next day in order to proceed to the Dardanelles.
Naturally I was overjoyed. No one could have been more heartily
tired of Lemnos than I, and I had hated the idea of being left out
of the show in which so many of my friends were to take part. The
next day I reported on board the flagship well before my time. On
the 23rd the transports began to weigh anchor and steam out of the
harbour. Everyone was much excited, and as the ships passed us
there were loud bursts of cheering. All were pleased to see the last of
Lemnos and to be up and doing. Some of the wags in the transports
had painted large white mottoes on the sides of their ships. One was
'Turkish Delight', another 'To Constantinople and the Harems'. We
(the *Euryalus*), together with the *Swiftsure* and *Implacable*, followed
the transports, leaving the harbour about 7 p.m. and arriving in the
open roadstead of Tenedos at daybreak the next morning.

The transports continued to come in during the night. The
famous *River Clyde* anchored close to us. She had been painted a dirty
khaki colour and certainly looked anything but smart. The *Queen
Elizabeth*, which arrived from Mudros shortly after us, reported that
she had passed within twenty-five yards of a floating mine, which
she had fired at and exploded. Several of these floating mines had
been sighted during the two previous weeks: they were apparently

drifting down from the Dardanelles. That same evening 900 men of the 1st Battalion Lancashire Fusiliers came on board, so we were a very crowded ship, and in the wardroom had to arrange two sittings for dinner. The soldiers fraternised with our Bluejackets, who put up a good supper for them. I heard one of the former remark that he had not had such good food since he left England.

During the night we all sailed for Gallipoli, and arrived off the coast – the very southernmost end – at 3.30 a.m. the next day, the 25th April, 1915. We, the *Euryalus*, were opposite to W Beach.

We all turned out early, and not without at least one rather humorous incident. Just alongside my cabin, a lot of hammocks had been slung, in which were sleeping not only Bluejackets but also some officers of the Lancashire Fusiliers. Of course, only the Bluejackets turned out on hearing the pipe, and the bos'n, coming along and seeing some men – sailors, as he thought – still lying in their hammocks, began to sing out, 'Show a leg there: show a leg.' Seeing no response to his order, he got justly enraged, and, rushing up to the nearest occupied hammock, with another bellow of 'Show a leg,' he gave the unfortunate occupant a hard punch in the back. Whereupon a Marine, who happened to be standing near, called out, 'Look out: that's an officer.' The bos'n gave one horrified glance at the angry face of the Major whom he had punched – and fled.

We made a very early breakfast and then went to our quarters. I had been told off to the after-turret: but as I thought that 1 should see nothing from there, I got out of it, and later was taken up on the flying bridge by the Captain. Just before going up, when I was walking forward along the deck, I met General Sir Hunter Weston. I saluted: he stopped and had a good look at me. At the time I was in a dirty old tunic and had on no badges of rank.

'What's your unit?' he asked, after he had said good morning. 'Well, sir,' I explained: 'I am a temporary officer lent by the Egyptian Government, attached to a French seaplane squadron, OC of a British ship carrying French 'planes which has been torpedoed and is ashore at Lemnos, and I am now on board the *Euryalus* by order of Admiral Wemyss as an Intelligence Officer.' The General looked very puzzled, but murmured, 'I see' – as I am perfectly sure he did not – smiled, and passed on.

On the bridge I was in the front stalls, so to speak: the only other people there being Admiral Wemyss, General Sir Hunter Weston and the Captain. I could see perfectly everything that happened. It was a lovely morning and the sea was absolutely calm with an early mist still hanging over it. This was a day never to be forgotten.

At 4.55 a.m. all the ships began to bombard the cliffs and the slope beyond. These ships – covering ships, as they were called – were the *Euryalus*, *Albion*, *Vengeance*, *Implacable*, *Nelson*, *Agamemnon*, *Cornwallis*, *Dublin*, etc.: the *Queen Elizabeth*, with Admiral de Robeck on board, being further up the coast.

The bombardment continued for about half an hour, and not a shot was fired by the enemy in reply. In fact, the cliffs and shore looked absolutely deserted.

By about 4 a.m. all the men had taken their places in the boats, and lay alongside the ships waiting for the order to push off: which was eventually given at 5.10. These troops were distributed to land as follows:

V Beach: 1st Munsters, 1st Dublins and two Companies of
    the 2nd Hampshires (from *River Clyde*).
W Beach: 1st Lancashire Fusiliers (4th Worcesters,
    V Beach), and one platoon 'Anson' Naval Brigade.
X Beach: 2nd R. Fusiliers and one platoon 'Anson' Brigade.
    Y Beach: Marine Division and K.O.S.B.s.
Z Beach: South Wales Borderers.
Further North: New Zealanders and Australians.

It was the landing at W Beach with which we were chiefly concerned. The men, as I have said, had all taken their places in the boats, and with each boatload were four Bluejackets, who were to remain as boat-minders when the soldiers disembarked.

At about a quarter-past five a fleet of small picquet boats took the loaded boats in tow – five each – and headed, line abreast, for the beach – a small sandy cove with cliffs on its two sides and a stiff slope up in front. It was a beautiful sight.

As the steamers neared the beach, the ships ceased fire: and once within 150 yards of the shore, the boats were cast adrift, when the soldiers got out their oars and raced each other for the beach. But the minute the boats started to row the silence was broken by a terrific rifle and machine-gun fire from the entrenched and concealed Turkish positions. The boats never hesitated although, packed as they were, the casualties were awful; they grounded, and our men leaped out, carrying their rifles with bayonets fixed, leaving many dead and wounded behind them. They waded ashore, many being tripped by strands of barbed-wire placed under water. A fiercer fire than ever was now opened upon them. I saw a row of 130 men bowled over as if by a single shot. There they lay, half in and half out of the water – eighty of them dead.

The wounded crawled on shore on their hands and knees. The survivors, however, never checked for a moment, but hacked their way through the barbed-wire entanglement with which the shore was covered, and charged the Turkish trenches and machine-guns, driving the enemy before them and storming the cliffs and slopes. The *Euryalus*, in the meanwhile, had steamed in within 1,000 yards of the beach, and now let fly with all her 6-inch that could be brought to bear on the retreating Turks, at the same time shelling with her forward 9·2 all the Turkish trenches that could be observed.

Nothing could have exceeded the gallantry of our men, both when rowing in and when storming the cliffs. No one hesitated: all went forward into what appeared to be certain death. As they hacked their way through the wire, I heard General Sir Hunter Weston, who was standing near me, exclaim involuntarily, 'Gallant fellows: gallant fellows.'

It was now about 7 a.m., and in the meantime some of the boats in which the dead and wounded were lying had drifted off the beach, either to be rowed by perhaps a couple of wounded men or to be taken in tow by the picquet boats and brought alongside the ship. They were a fearful sight – dead and wounded all jumbled up together in their bottoms, and there the wretched men had to lie, as everybody on board was busy shelling the Turks and sending off more boatloads of whole men to reinforce those already landed. I myself heard the Commander ask the Admiral if he was to hoist the wounded inboard, and the Admiral, one of the kindest-hearted men in the service, say, 'No, they are out of action and no use at present. Our first duty is to reinforce the men on shore, so that they can hang on to what they have gained.' And he was right. Unless we had sent reinforcements, our men on shore who were hanging on by their eyelids might have been swept back into the sea and the whole campaign ended in a fiasco.

Later in the day, I was told that one of the 'boat-minders', who, finding himself the only live man in his boat, seized a rifle and charged with the soldiers, saved a Brigadier-General, and captured a machine-gun 'on his own'. I asked Captain Burmester what reward this man would be given if the tale proved to be true. The answer was short and to the point: 'I don't know anything about a *reward*, but what he will be given will be a damned good telling-off for leaving his boat without orders.'

By 8 a.m. our landing-party had joined hands with the Royal Fusiliers, who had landed at X Beach: and, seeing that our position W Beach had been made good, we – the *Euryalus* – steamed towards W Beach to assist as we could. This is what had occurred there. At 7 a.m. the tramp-steamer, *River Clyde* (which as I have already mentioned, had been specially fitted out for this work, all cargo having been taken out of her and large openings, from which gangways were slung, cut in her sides), steamed in under a full head of steam and ran ashore under the fort of Sudd-el-Bahr. Roughly 2,000 troops were on board her. Having bumped the beach, she pushed ahead the decked barges or lighters which she had been towing, lowered her gangways on to them, and so formed a connecting-link with the shore. Immediately the men – Dublins and Munsters – led by their officers, charged down these gangways. A terrific machine-gun and rifle fire was opened on them from the Turkish trenches, which were within a few yards of the beach, and also from concealed nests in the old fort and town of Sudd-el-Bahr. I could see the wretched men being swept off the gangways and lighters in hundreds. Some, indeed, managed to reach the shore and took cover under the low cliff, or, rather, steep bank which fringed it. Many of these towards the western end were enfiladed and killed. General Hunter Weston, the GOC on our ship, signalled to the troops, congratulating them, and saying that England expected them to hold the position to the last man. I don't suppose for one minute that the message was ever taken in by the men who were fighting for their lives under that bit of cliff. I heard later that the Dublins and Munsters lost 750 out of 1,900 men. There were no officers of the Dublins left and only five of the Munsters. It was, however, only a rumour that the two battalions were amalgamated and called 'The Royal Dumsters'.

The greatest number of casualties amongst the Dublins and Munsters occurred when, as they were charging across the barges linking the *River Clyde* to the shore, one of the lighters broke adrift. Seeing this happen, Commander Unwin and Midshipman Drewry stripped and swam from the ship to the lighter in question and, under a terrific fire, managed to get her into her proper position again. They were both awarded the VC, as were also Midshipman Mallison and Samson, AB, who assisted them, for this gallant action.

Soon afterwards some more boatloads of troops pulled in to V Beach, but were practically annihilated as they landed: and shortly after this, while the Dubs and Munsters were lighting desperately to keep their footing on the shore, I noticed a whole fleet of boats being towed in towards them. These were the Worcesters, who, according to former orders, were to be landed as soon as the troops from the *River Clyde* had made good their position on the beach. They were going in to a certain death – no one could have said that the landing had been made good. It looked so awful that I took the bull by the horns and called the Admiral's attention. He had a look through his glasses and spoke to the General. After a few minutes, I had the satisfaction of seeing a signal being made to the boats diverting them to W Beach, where the Lancashire Fusiliers had certainly made good their landing. I felt nervous butting in on what was not my business, and I might have been badly snubbed. But I was not, and I have never been sorry that I risked it.

The French in the meantime were attacking the Asiatic side of the Straits, near the sight of ancient Troy. The idea was that the French battleships should engage the forts near Kum Kali, and so prevent these from joining with their friends on the Peninsula in an attack on our landing-parties. The French battleships were a little late in tackling their job. But they did bring it off, and a French force landed under cover of their guns and took several forts. This attack was of the greatest assistance to our forces at Sudd-el-Bahr, as the French kept the enemy so busy that they were unable to shell our landing-party effectively. In fact, only two shells hit the *River Clyde*.

As darkness set in the position at V Beach was as follows. A good many Dublins, Munsters and Hampshires held the beach, crouching for cover at the base of a low cliff. The remainder of the troops were still in the *River Clyde*, and the OC decided to wait until it was quite dark before attempting to land them. Hundreds of lives were saved by his decision.

By this time the sea near the shore was a red blood-colour, which could be seen hundreds of yards away. The casualties had been enormous. In my opinion, there is no doubt that if only one opening in the *River Clyde* had been made, and this in the stem ('sharp end') – and that if the gangways and lighters had been protected by plates of sheet iron, the troops could have been landed with very little loss. However . . .

We received news in the evening that the Australians had landed successfully further up the coast, but the night was a very anxious one for all of us. It was pitch dark and raining, and there was a continuous roar of musketry. Things at one time seemed so bad we received orders to keep all available boats ready in case it was found necessary to evacuate. Thank goodness day broke without the need for such an attempt. One can imagine what an awful business it would have been in the dark with the enemy attacking, and one dreaded to think of the awful casualties we must have incurred.

On the morning of the 26th the Lancashires, Royal Fusiliers and Worcesters made good their positions, and our line ran continuously from X to W Beaches. The Worcesters then proceeded to attack some strongly held trenches which were to the east of the line on the cross of the ridge running west to east between W and V Beaches. By occupying them it was hoped to join hands with the troops landed at V, and thus to extend our line right across the Peninsula from sea to sea. The attack by the Worcesters was superbly carried out in rushes, while we shelled the enemy's trenches with our 9·2-inch and 6-inch guns. The troops would charge a short way, then lie down and lay out a large red flag on the ground to mark their position for us. We then shelled: after a few minutes the red flag would be rolled up: we ceased firing, they charged and lay down again, and so on. The red flag was a very necessary precaution. The previous day one of our shells had burst right on a party of our men and had knocked out many of them. When the Worcesters were close to the enemy's trenches they prepared for their final charge. But between them and their objective was a barbed-wire entanglement. Nothing daunted, up got three men – I couldn't see if they were officers or men – and calmly walked about cutting the wire with their nippers, just as if they were cutting roses in a garden, the Turks blazing away at them all the time. I saw two of them bowled over, but others took their place. We, in the meanwhile, were shelling the trench hard. The *Triumph* – or was it the *Swiftsure*? – landed a beauty right in the trench. At once the red flag was rolled up and a wild charge was made. I could see the men on top of the trench, and then they sprang into it with their bayonets and it was ours. It was splendidly done, and a most spectacular affair for those looking on.

During the last night the OC of the troops in the *River Clyde* had managed to land the rest of his men – about a thousand – and these, joining the rest on the beach, worked round the shore to Sudd-el-Bahr village and fought their way into it. So the Dublins, Munsters and Rants proceeded to advance up the slope towards the old castle which was at the top of the ridge to the east of the redoubt the Worcesters had just taken. Colonel Dought-Wylie, of the Staff, gallantly led the men, and most of their own officers were *hors de combat*. They cleared the village of snipers and gradually worked their way up the slope, taking trench after trench by short rushes, till in the afternoon they took the old castle itself at the point of the bayonet, and held it, firing on the Turks, who retreated down the other side of the ridge. They now joined hands with the Worcesters, and we held a continuous line across the Peninsula. That evening we all fell in on the quarterdeck and buried seventeen of our poor fellows over the side. The service was most impressive. The dead were sewn up in canvas and laid in a row on the deck, the service read, and then one by one they were placed on a plank, and at the word of command 'lift', were slid over the side. I noticed a row of about ten Turkish prisoners on deck watching with great interest.

Our casualties were estimated at about 2,000. We did not take many prisoners: in fact, I believe the Dublins and Munsters took none, and I don't blame them. It appeared that when they eventually got possession of Sudd-el-Bahr town they found several of their dead indescribably mutilated. One wretched man while still alive had been trussed up and placed on a charcoal fire, another was found with a bayonet stuck right through his cheeks, one had his tongue cut out, several were disembowelled, etc. Shortly after seeing these the Dubs and Munsters captured some snipers and two German officers and just killed them off-hand – and they swore they wouldn't take any more prisoners alive.

Amongst our killed was the padre, Father Finn, a most gallant man. He insisted on landing with his men from the *River Clyde*, and went round all the morning attending to the wounded and dying under heavy fire. He was first of all wounded and then killed. Next morning, the 27th, we were busy shelling the Turks and bringing off wounded to the ships. By some misunderstanding we had arrived with only one hospital ship – the *Sudan* – all the others having been left at Mudros. The consequence was that the wounded had to be taken on board any ship that had room. We actually had 300, and only the two ship's surgeons to attend to them: these officers, in consequence, were nearly worn out.

Personally, I was occupied all day in looking after the 'spotting map' on the bridge. When a signal was received saying an enemy's gun, trench or body of troops had been observed on such a position on the map, it was my business to find it and point it out to the Admiral.

The French now evacuated Kum Kali on the Asiatic side, and were brought over and landed at V Beach to reinforce the right wing, which had been till now held by the greatly depleted Dubs and Munsters. As it turned out, the evacuation of the Asiatic side was a mistake, as the Turks mounted heavy guns there and began (and continued) to shell the beaches the whole time we remained on the Peninsula.

The French troops were colonials, and amongst them were some of the 'Foreign Legion'. One day a boatload of the latter passed our ship, and our men were shouting greetings to them, when one of them called out to a stout Bluejacket, 'S'long, Tubby – see you again shortly', thus proving that there was anyway one Englishman amongst them.

A naval division was landed at W Beach and the troops from Y Beach were brought around and landed there too. Apparently they had been roughly handled at Y Beach and were doing no good there. Our troops now advanced down the northern slope of the ridge towards the village of Krithia. We were continuously shelling Krithia and Achi Baba. When we were firing one always had to keep cotton wool in the ears, and funnily enough the 6-inch guns had more effect on the hearing than the large 9·2-inch.

One morning while I was on the bridge, a petty officer, who had been gazing over the side, asked me if I knew what a mine was like. I ran to the end of the bridge, and was horrified to see what to all appearances was a floating mine within five yards of the ship. While I was looking at it it suddenly moved and disappeared – it was a great big turtle. The same morning the cap of a small signal-boy who was standing beside me (he was only about fourteen years old) was suddenly knocked off his head. He stooped down, and as he was picking it up, out fell a bullet. It was evidently a spent bullet and had struck the thick wadding of the cap. The yeoman of signals, hearing a surprised exclamation from the boy, turned round and said, 'What's the matter?' 'I 'ave been struck by a bullet,' replied the boy. 'Oh, 'ave you? Well, carry on,' was all the sympathy he got from the busy yeoman. I told the boy to keep the bullet, but warned him no one was likely to believe the yarn, although it was absolutely true.

On the morning of the 28th we heard that the *Queen Elizabeth* had sunk a Turkish transport by indirect fire right over the Peninsula, a seaplane spotting for her. She also practically wiped out a whole battalion of Turks who were on the march. Her shells weighed a ton and contained, I believe, 30,000 bullets the size of small marbles. The same morning I went ashore to try and find a quick-firing gun lent to the soldiers by our ship. I rowed alongside the *River Clyde* and clambered on board. All her sides were pitted with bullets, and even then the Turks on the Asiatic side were shelling her and V Beach. I climbed down on to the lighters and got ashore. Here a party of men were busy dragging the sea round the ship and close to the shore for the bodies of the unfortunate men who while landing had been hit and, falling off the gangways and lighters, were drowned, if not already dead, as they were loaded with their full equipment. I never could understand why they were not landed at first with only their rifles and ammunition – the rest of their kit could have been sent to them after they had made good their landing: and a lot of the slightly wounded who fell into the sea might then possibly have saved themselves by swimming.

I went up over the trenches lately occupied by live Turks (they were now occupied by dead ones), towards the old castle on the ridge summit. It was not altogether pleasant, as there were still a few snipers concealed in the town who had occasional pots at anyone exposing himself. A little way up I came across a Dublin sitting smoking with his back against a rock. His leg was badly shattered, the bone sticking out through the skin. He had bound it up as well as he could. I stopped and spoke to him for a bit and told him not to let anyone remove his bandage till he was safely on board a hospital ship, where he could get proper attention, or else he ran a risk of tetanus. He was quite cheerful, and when I said I was sorry for him, he replied, 'Shure, sir, and am n't I better off than them poor boys?' pointing to about thirty dead Dubs and Munsters lying close to him. A little farther on, behind a rock in front of a Turkish trench, I came upon two hands of playing cards laid out on the ground. Apparently two men had had a quiet (?) hand of 'Nap' while awaiting the order to charge the trench. The French were in occupation of the old castle and the Turks were shelling it, so I did not remain any longer than necessary, and after some time climbed down the slope and went towards the shore.

On the 30th April a German aeroplane flew over us and dropped bombs, which, however, fell wide, exploding in the water. We were busy shelling all day, and heard in the evening that the *Lord Nelson*, which had been shelling Chanak, had been lucky enough to set it on fire. We were all greatly relieved to see several transports, arriving full of reinforcements. These were Indian troops under command of General Cox, whom I had met in Port Said, and on the 12th May they were landed on the Peninsula.

Things were soon looking considerably more healthy, and we began to take a brighter view of existence.

About this time an amusing incident occurred on board the *Euryalus*. There was a custom in the wardroom of tossing with dice for drinks. One evening some of us were doing this when the Admiral came in, and, after looking on for a bit through his eye-glass, turned to the Commander, and said: 'I have a sort of recollection, Jack, that there is some regulation forbidding this.' 'Yes, sir,' replied the Commander, 'but we pay no attention to it in this ship,' and continued to toss.

6

Back to the Aenne

May–July, 1915

B Y THIS TIME I had got used to life on board the *Euryalus*, and it was something of a shock when the Captain sent for me and told me that he had received a message from Colonel Elgood, Base Commander, Port Said, to the effect that I was to return to Egypt with the *Aenne Rickmers* as soon as the latter was in a fit state to return anywhere. Personally I had no desire to resume my wanderings and was very keen to stay where I was. But as I really belonged to General Maxwell's force there was no escaping the order, and on the 4th May I boarded the *Dago*, a small ship of the Wilson Line, sailing that evening for Lemnos. I was very sorry to leave the *Euryalus*, for from the Admiral down to the 'Snotties' everyone had treated me most kindly.

I had never met any of the *Dago*'s crew before. This fact led to rather an odd incident. It happened just after I had left the Captain, with whom I had been chatting, to go to bed. I had to pass through a small saloon on the way to my cabin, and there I ran into a couple of men who I took to be ship's officers. They nodded to me affably as I came up to them, and asked me to have a drink. I accepted the offer, and spent a few cheerful minutes with them. Then I turned in. Judge my surprise, therefore, when the next morning I recognised the man who brought in my cup of tea and took my boots to clean as one of my hospitable friends of the night before. He was perfectly polite, and made no attempt to remind me of our late informal acquaintance, but I could not help wondering what would have happened if the Captain had seen me drinking whisky (most likely his whisky) with two of his stewards. We arrived at Mudros at dawn on 5th May, and I reported my arrival on board the *Hussar*. At first I was told that I should be sent on to Egypt in the first ship sailing there, but later this information was contradicted, and in the midst of a perfect hail of confused orders I made for the old *Aenne*, where I was welcomed with open arms by Bishop, who had had a remarkably dull time during my absence.

The next day Captain Hayes Sadler, late Captain of HMS *Ocean*, and then SNO, Mudros, came on board. He told us that, as soon as we were patched up, we were to be given the original crew of the *River Clyde*, with whom we were to set off and try to reach Alexandria, where we could be docked. The big repair ship *Reliance* had taken charge of us, and at last it looked as if there was some hope of the poor old *Aenne* being repaired. To get some exercise, Bishop and I went ashore for a stroll, and walked over to the little picturesque village of Portiana, about four miles distant. It was a quaint old village lying amongst vine and barley fields, and the inhabitants seemed quite pleased to see us, and presented us with roses and carnations.

Next day, while out for a walk along the shore, we came across the body of a Greek fisherman who had been drowned. While we were still near the Greek police arrived, dug a hole in the sand and buried him there – no service or anything, just as if he were a dog. Queer people!

On the 9th May Bishop and I went on board the *Reliance* to lunch with Captain Williams. He showed us all over her. She certainly was a wonderful ship, nothing more nor less than an enormous workshop. Down in her hold one could not realise he was on board a ship. It was like being in a big foundry.

On the 10th May I again went on board the *Hussar*, where I was told definitely that Captain Gaskell was not coming back to the *Aenne Rickmers* and that we were to be sent Captain Kerr, late of the *River Clyde*, at any rate for the voyage to Alexandria. While on board the *Hussar* I heard the news that a German submarine had got into the Mediterranean. This was the beginning of submarine warfare in our part of the world.

By the time I got back to the *Aenne* our new skipper had arrived. He was a real good sort, a Scot from the island of Arran. He could talk Gaelic, and when excited always spoke with an appalling Yankee accent. He had been at sea ever since he was thirteen, and had been skipper of 'wind-jammers', salvage ships and tramp- steamers. Thus he had seen every part of the world and, amongst other things, had once been for a short time in the American cavalry. Bishop and I were delighted to have him with us as we had long ago exhausted all our best stories and he was chock-a-block with tales we had never heard.

On the 12th May our 'hole' was at last finished, and at 8.30 a.m. our new crew came on board. They were a fine, tough-looking lot, all sorts of nationalities, but, thank goodness, no Greeks. The bos'n was an enormous Irishman, and the majority of the others were Scandinavians. All the officers and engineers were Scots with the exception of 'the second', who was an Australian, Lieutenant Buck, from Kangaroo Island.

About 10.30 a.m. a tug took us in tow and pulled us off the beach without much effort. This was a great moment. We were actually afloat once again, and had even got steam up. We were all delighted.

On the 14th May, after taking in fresh water from a collier that came alongside, we weighed anchor, and sailed at 11 a.m., in company with a hospital ship that was proceeding to Malta. Having heard that the enemy's submarines were somewhere in the neighbourhood, we naturally kept an extra good look out, not that we could have done anything if one appeared, for our full speed was only a wretched ten knots, and our armament consisted of a few service rifles.

On the 15th we passed the islands of Scarpanto and Rhodes, and also a big western ocean ship, the transport *California*, on her way to Gallipoli crammed with troops. There was a big swell, and we soon began to take water in through our patch. The next morning we sent a wireless asking for two tugs to meet us outside Alexandria harbour to tow us through the Pass. During the night we had taken about 600 tons of water into our No. 1 hold, and we were steering badly. The tugs, however, came out and towed us safely into port. That morning I went ashore, reported to the Ports and Lights and Administration, and introduced the new captain. The next few days I spent in trying to persuade the Ports and Lights to engage our temporary crew from the *River Clyde* permanently for the *Aenne*. They made very heavy weather about this, and said Greeks would be cheaper, whereupon I kicked, pointing out that our late experience of Greeks had not made me keen to try another lot of them.

Eventually I went off to Cairo in the hopes of getting the military authorities there to order the Ports and Lights to engage the crew I wanted. This I did successfully, and I congratulated myself on having settled the crew difficulty once and for all. Unfortunately, as I found soon afterwards, my congratulations were somewhat premature. But of that later.

While I was in Cairo – I was staying at the Turf Club – I received a telephone message to say that General Maxwell wanted to see me at GHQ. I was shaving at the time, and I had to get a move on to be in time. I dashed down, couldn't find a belt – Sam Browne – so took the first I saw in the hall, and away I went. I was shown into a room where were the General's two ADCs, Prince Alexander of Battenburg and the Marquis of Anglesea – and after a short time was taken in to the General himself. He was charming, and asked me to tell him all about my experience when the ship was torpedoed. I showed him some photos of the 'hole' and he froze on to them. Then he asked me what I thought of the 'landing' on the morning of the 25th April at Gallipoli. I said, 'Well, sir, it was pretty–' 'Bloody,' he remarked. I agreed, and then described to him what I had seen and knew about it. He appeared to be most interested.

That afternoon I returned to Alexandria, and the next morning the second round of my struggle with the Ports and Lights began. The Director-General informed me that Captain Gaskell had arrived, and that he was to take command of the *Aenne* as before. This annoyed me considerably, as I knew that Gaskell had parted 'brass rags' with the French seaplane commandant and that the latter would refuse to put his 'planes on board the ship if Gaskell was to be captain. I explained this to the Director-General, and then, after some further argument, clinched the business by telling him that the military authorities in Cairo had agreed to take on Captain Kerr and his crew, and had ordered me to say so. The matter was then reconsidered.

All this time – and up to the middle of June – the *Aenne* was in dry dock being properly repaired. Every day I used to go on board and see what progress had been made; but otherwise I had a good deal of spare time on my hands, so that I was able to look up a fair number of friends. I remember that once, when I was dining at the Union Club, I ran into Mr Preston. He was the president of the Prize Court, and was responsible for the cargo on board the *Aenne*, and he at once tackled me about this. He had heard all sorts of rumours about what had happened to us – and to the precious cargo. The fate of the latter naturally interested him most, and he was greatly relieved when I assured him that it was all right. Soon afterwards we discharged that £250,000 worth of cargo, as the authorities came to the conclusion that it was not worthwhile allowing us to carry it as ballast. I don't blame them.

There was an American cruiser in the harbour all this time. Her crew were not very popular with our men, and as America was still standing out of the war, 'too proud to fight' was frequently quoted at them. This naturally led to a good many scraps, which enlivened the harbour quite a little. When she was about to sail, an old Irishman, O'Sullivan, who was harbour master, or harbour pilot, went on board to take her out. Later he told me what happened. He stepped up on the bridge, saluted the Captain and introduced himself with 'My name is O'Sullivan.' 'And mine is Sc...', mentioning a typical German name, replied the American. 'Sounds German,' said O'Sullivan without thinking. 'Well, I am German,' shouted the furious American. O'Sullivan was glad when he had finished his job and could get away.

On 28th May our seaplane party, including Herbert, Hillas and de Saizieu, turned up from Tenedos, where they had been landed by the *Rabenfels*. They had practically commandeered some old tramp-steamer to get across. I was glad to see them again, and we all felt that it was quite like old times.

The next morning, as the *Aenne* was still in dry dock, I went off to Port Said, where I called at Navy House.

There I saw Commander Thursifield, who told me that we – the *Aenne Rickmers* – were to be commissioned, were to fly the White Ensign, and that the Captain and officers – including the chief engineer – were to be given RNR commissions, and that junior engineers were to be given warrant rank. This was good news. It meant that the ship was going to be run by the 'pukka' navy, and not by the Ports and Lights Administration, under orders from GOC, Egypt, which latter arrangement had proved absolutely unworkable, as far as the ship's officers and crew were concerned. At last, on the 18th June, the old *Aenne*, thoroughly repaired, came out of dock and anchored in the Arsenal basin. It was then that we discharged our cargo. This left us without ballast, and I wrote to the naval authorities at Port Said suggesting that I should be allowed to fill the hold of the ship with watertight barrels. I stated that if I got permission I would purchase these barrels locally. My idea was to have sand ballast, and on top of this and also 'tween decks, to put the watertight barrels, so making the ship practically unsinkable, even if torpedoed. But I never got any reply to my letter and the scheme fell through, although I believe it was tried later in the war with satisfactory results.

The next few days were spent in doing minor repairs (and I took the opportunity of having my cabin double-lined to keep out the cold), and on the 30th June we sailed for Port Said, where we arrived next morning after a voyage made thoroughly uncomfortable by lack of ballast.

It was now that the crew difficulty, which, as I have hinted earlier, had never been properly settled, became acute. Although we had taken on the officers – or rather most of them – of the *River Clyde* while still in Alexandria, the crew had refused to stay, and we had come round to Port Said with a makeshift of Kroo boys, who on arrival had to be sent back to their ships. Naturally we appealed to the authorities, but little help was forthcoming from that direction. The Navy sent us a signalman and five Bluejackets who were to 'man' the steamboat, but otherwise we were simply told that we must raise a crew for ourselves. Well, we set about it. We got firemen all right. And at last we even got a crew of sorts. They were the sweepings of Port Said, and I don't think any of them – with one exception – had ever been on a ship before, except perhaps to carry coal on board. The bos'n had been to sea years ago on a Khedival boat – that's why he was made bos'n – but as he had been working as bash suffragi (head waiter) in the Eastern Exchange Hotel for the past four years he was a bit out of practice. I doubt if any ship ever sailed with such a crew since the days of the Ark.

But sail we did. At 8 p.m. on the 7th July we managed to get our anchor up and proceeded to sea, taking with us a couple of seaplanes. There had been a report that a submarine had been seen off Borollos, and it was our business to steam along the coast and search for it with our 'planes. But we saw nothing, so hoisted the 'planes on board and made towards Aboukir Bay. We meant to search the bay with a 'plane, but the sea was too rough to hoist it out, so I decided to go into Alexandria Harbour, hoist out the 'plane there and let it fly to Aboukir. This we did – with unexpected results. For just after our 'plane had returned a staff officer arrived on board in great excitement to enquire what we meant by flying there without having informed the authorities. I told him that I had asked the naval authorities at Port Said to inform Alexandria that we were going to fly in that vicinity, but apparently they had forgotten to do so. The consequence was that when our 'plane flew over Ras-el-Tin and the Ramleh shore, it was taken for a German and created quite a mild panic. In fact we heard afterwards that two coastguards had let off their rifles at her. So we returned to Port Said feeling like injured martyrs.

On the 17th I was sent for by the French Admiral, d'Artige Fournier, and given orders for a cruise which he wanted us to make in company with French warships. Next day I had to meet the morning train from Cairo and receive a despatch from the American Consul-General, with which I was ordered to sail at once, to deliver it in person to the US cruiser *Des Moines*, supposed to be lying at Beirut. Before leaving I wrote to Colonel Elgood and said I thought it only fair to put in writing a statement setting forth the conditions in which we were sailing, namely, with a crew consisting chiefly of *fellahin*, no steamboat – it had been taken away – and hardly a man in the ship who could pull a boat, no one capable of taking the wheel with the exception of the ship's officers, and entirely unarmed except for a few revolvers. I pointed out that we should have 'pukka' naval ratings for our crew, and that also we ought to have a steamboat, a Maxim and a 12-pounder, as we knew that there were enemy submarines in the area in which we had to operate. The fact was that we were 'nobody's child': but, serving under the British Army, British Navy and French Navy, we could get nothing out of any of them except orders, and we got plenty of those. I thought it advisable to write all this before sailing in case anything happened to us.

7

Coastal Work

July–September, 1915

WE SAILED AT midnight on July 18th. It was a case of getting back to our old work. For the next twelve months we were cruising up and down the coast of Syria and Asia Minor, landing and embarking our agents, sending off our 'planes to reconnoitre, and generally doing the hundred and one odd jobs that the powers thought fit to give us. It was like the days before the *Aenne* had been torpedoed all over again – and yet only superficially like. However similar to others it may seem in the telling, each incident of that period had a character of its own; to each its own excitement, boredom, humour, or even terror. Looking through the pages of the diary which I then kept, I can find little which has not at least a personal interest: and it is only with the greatest difficulty that I can decide what episodes to leave out in the present narrative. Even as it is, I fear that the reader will find that I have left more than enough, but if so he can always indulge in the gentle art of 'skipping'.

To begin with – I did not deliver any despatches to the *Des Moines*. We came up with her off Beirut easily enough, and signalled to her. She did not reply. So I wirelessed: but although I stated that the despatches were from the American Consul-General, the only answer I could get was a repeated, 'Impossible to communicate with you.' There was no fear of her breaking her strict neutrality. All I could do was to wireless to HQ for instructions. When these were forthcoming, I gathered that the despatches could not have been so important after all, as I was simply told to retain them and continue the cruise.

On the 21st July we received a message from the French flagship, the *Jeanne d'Arc*, ordering us to rendezvous with her in Pegodia Bay, Island of Scarpanto. Off we went and, arriving the same afternoon, found the *Jeanne d'Arc* awaiting us. I boarded her, saw the Admiral, and received my instructions, which were that the *Aenne* was to accompany the flagship on a trip along the Asia Minor coast in order that our 'planes might be used to reconnoitre for submarine bases.

Accordingly, off Delaman Chai ('chai' is Turkish for river) I sent away a 'plane, which returned after an hour and a half's flight and reported nothing suspicious. So we steamed off to Makri, where I sent away a 'plane with Trouillet and Herbert, who dropped bombs on the Turkish barracks and returned to the ship. This meant another trip to the Admiral, who, when I had reported, told me that if while we were cruising in company either the *Jeanne d'Arc* or the *Aenne* were submarined, the other ship was not to stop and pick up survivors, but was to steam away at full speed, adopting a zigzag course. I talked this over with our captain, and we both agreed that as we should not have much chance of escaping (we could then only do nine knots), we might as well zigzag around the victim, rescue anybody we could and trust to luck. Luckily we did not have to put this plan into practice. I might mention here that when at sea in company with the French flagship, after any of our 'planes had made a flight, I had always to proceed on board the flagship to inform the Admiral of the result. This necessitated my putting on my best uniform and helmet and steaming over in our launch. I then had to climb on board by an iron ladder, and as the French ships burnt briquettes, I arrived on the deck with jet-black hands. However, as every French officer I met on my way to the Admiral's cabin saluted and shook hands with me, I was quite unsoiled when I met him. I was rather puzzled at first as to the proper method of proceeding on entering his cabin. Being in military uniform, I should have kept my helmet on, but naval officers, on entering a superior officer's cabin, take off theirs and put them under their left arm. I got out of the difficulty by entering the cabin with helmet on, saluted, and then took it off and put it under my arm: so I think we were all pleased.

We arrived at Rhodes next day and found besides the *Jeanne d'Arc* an Italian man-o'-war and the American ship *Des Moines*, which we had last seen off Beirut. We went on shore and had a look round the town, a most picturesque old place surrounded by ancient walls and towers. We went over the Museum, which was formerly the fortress of the Knights of Rhodes. It was in a fine state of preservation. The Italians were in possession of the island, which they had taken from the Turks three years before our visit. They certainly had made a good clean job of the town, and everything was in perfect order. Wherever we went we were followed by a crowd of children gazing at our strange uniforms – for we all wore 'shorts'. The people seemed to be a mixture of races: Turks, Italians, Hebrews and Greeks. The roads were very good and there was quite a respectable harbour for small craft – though we lay outside. The island was full of Italian troops.

We returned on board and sailed at 3 p.m. for the Bay of Marmarice to search for more submarine bases – which we did not find. In the days before the war the Mediterranean Squadron used to rendezvous there to coal from colliers. It is a magnificent harbour surrounded by high hills. In fact, all this part of the Asia Minor coast is very picturesque and is backed with high, forest-covered mountains. Many of the foot-hills are crowned with castles dating back to the time of the Crusades. Taking it all together it would be a splendid cruising ground for a small yacht in peace time, and one would get the best of shooting there as well. After a few more fruitless flights, I went again to see the Admiral. He was a most charming man and seemed pleased with the negative results of our reconnaisances. He said that we had proved the rumours of submarine bases on this coast to be false. The *Jeanne d'Arc* then sailed for Port Said, and left us to waddle there by ourselves. We arrived safely and landed our seaplanes. Next day I went on board the *Jeanne d'Arc* and had a first-class lunch with the Admiral.

The next three weeks or so we spent in port. There were various matters of 'interior economy' to attend to, especially as I heard that at last we were to get rid of our scratch crew. Get rid of most of them we did – but not quite in the way we had expected. For they went in a burst of glory – and some under arrest. What happened was that one day they amused themselves by getting up a regular battle amongst themselves, and we had to signal to HMS *Proserpine*, who sent over some naval ratings and arrested the ringleaders.

At this time our old ship was in luck's way, for we were actually given a 12-pounder and, best of all, on the 5th August we were ordered to haul down the Red Ensign and hoist the White. The former German cargo-boat, the *Aenne Rickmers*, had now become His Majesty's ship *Anne*.

On the 20th we sailed again and proceeded to Haifa Bay. With us were the *Jeanne d'Arc* and the French battleship *Jaureguiberry*. We received a signal to follow them, and we all steamed close in towards the shore. The *Jaureguiberry* then fired two heavy shells at the railway station which, as far as we could see, demolished it. Immediately afterwards we separated from the French and laid our course for Cyprus. The next morning we sighted a small schooner running northwards along the coast. We pursued her, and when she saw us, she ran in towards the shore so as to get into shoal water, where we could not follow her. To make her heave to we fired a shot from our 12-pounder across her bows. This shot ricocheted off the water and burst in the midst of some Turkish cavalry on shore, knocking a good many out – an unexpected, but welcome, bag for us. The schooner hauled down her sails signifying she surrendered, and we sent a boat's crew to bring her alongside. She was Turkish all right, and hailed from the Island of Ruad, near Tripoli. We took her in tow and proceeded to Famagusta, in Cyprus, where we arrived next morning and anchored about half a mile off the mouth of the harbour.

The harbour and the town, with its massive walls and towers, have much the same appearance as Rhodes. One tower was pointed out to us as being Othello's. Inside the walls there are the ruins of three hundred churches and chapels dating back to the time of the Crusaders. The largest church is in good repair and is used as a mosque. It is very fine and not unlike Rheims Cathedral. Most of the inhabitants inside the walls were Turks, the Greeks living outside.

We went and had meals in the little English club and were most kindly treated by its members. In the visitors' book at the club we were shown the names of the German Admiral and of the Captain of the *Goeben*, which had called there only a few days before the war broke out.

In the afternoon of the 17th we sailed for the Bay of Alexandretta. Here we met the *Jeanne d'Arc* and the *Raven* (formerly known as the *Rabenfels*). It was too stormy for a flight, so we had to wait until the next morning, when we went into the Gulf of Tarsus and hoisted out both our 'planes. Grall and Fletcher, Herbert and Destrem flew in ours: and de Saizieu and Ledger, Trouillet and Paul flew in the *Raven*'s. Shortly afterwards the *Raven*'s returned and reported that they could see nothing owing to the mist. Grall and Fletcher, however, were away two hours, and on their return reported that they had bombed the station of Adana. This was a good piece of work.

We then proceeded to the Gulf of Alexandretta and in the morning attempted a bombing flight to Osmanieh. Destrem and Herbert were in the machine, but after they had made several unsuccessful attempts to get off the water, we had to hoist them on board again. Destrem was much disgusted and excited. He rushed up to me and said, 'Weldon, I do not like going round and round like what you call dog with rabies, but I do try to conserve my hair!' The fact was that he was a heavy man and, the bombs being also weighty, the 80-hp engine was not powerful enough to lift the machine.

It would be merely boring to mention the names of all the places we visited on this and the succeeding cruises, but I remember that on the 21st August we joined the French warships, *Jeanne d'Arc*, *Destres* and the *Amiral Charnier* in St George's Bay, Beirut. This bay is one of the loveliest in the world. It is surrounded on three sides by thickly wooded hills which rise in a succession of ridges to the peaks of the Lebanon, while here and there from amongst the trees on the hillside peep the red-tiled roofs and the white stone walls of some wealthy merchant's summer villa. Beirut itself is, as I learnt later, an ordinary, rather dirty Levantine town: but not far away, perched on a ridge of the foot-hills and overlooking the bay, is the tiny village of Brumana, which James Elroy Flecker made famous by his poems. At this time, however, Brumana was as inaccessible to us as the heights of Thibet, and we had to content ourselves with steaming in fairly close to the harbour. In doing this, we passed not far from a sunken ship whose funnel and masts showed above water. This was the *Peter Rickmers*, owned by the same company as the *Aenne*, and had been sunk on purpose to prevent her falling into our hands. As we steamed by, I could not help thinking of the Bovril Co.'s advertisement, 'Alas, my poor brother.'

We sent away a 'plane with Destrem and Fletcher (as the observer), who returned safely, having made a good flight over the Damascus railway as far as Ain el Sofar. They had been heavily fired on and had had a narrow shave. One bullet would have got the observer if it had not been diverted by striking a pipe just beside him. When we sent and reported to the Admiral, he told me that he was going to recommend Fletcher and Herbert for the Croix de Guerre. We then sailed for Port Said, but had still another little adventure before we arrived safely in port. On rounding Ras el Beirut we saw a schooner making for shore: so we chased her and fired a shot to make her heave to. She did not heave to, but ran ashore instead. We let her crew get clear and then destroyed her with a few shots from our 12-pounder.

On arriving at Port Said I hurried on to Cairo and went carefully over all the maps of Sinai found on Turkish prisoners, with the idea of seeing if they had got hold of any of the 'confidential' maps of that district which had been made in the years previous to the war. Apparently they had not. This was curious, as I recollected that amongst others working on these maps in the Survey of Egypt, there had been a first-class German draughtsman!

Even in port life was not entirely uneventful. Once it was more the reverse than I liked. For one day I went for a flight with de l'Escaille to see if we could spot mines off the coast. After we had been up for about three-quarters of an hour I noticed that the petrol gauge only showed a centimetre of petrol. I drew de l'Escaille's attention to this and he at once headed for home. However, while we were over the land to the west of the town we ran out and dived down suddenly, landing with a severe bump in a small pond about 150 yards square. It appeared that the mechanic had forgotten to fill No. 1 tank! We pumped some petrol from No. 2 into No. 1 and then started to get off again. This was a ticklish job in such a small pond with a depth of only two feet. We just managed, however, to rise without hitting the shore. I don't believe we were more than three feet up when we reached the edge of the water, and I know I shut my eyes thinking we should hit the land and be turned head over heels. But all's well that ends well, and we got safely back to the Canal.

We sailed again on the 30th August, taking with us twenty-nine Turkish prisoners, all over military age. They were mostly sailors of captured schooners and came from the island of Ruad, near Tripoli, on the Syrian coast, and our orders were to repatriate them.

On the 31st August we did a flight over El Arish and then sailed for Ruad, and found the *Jeanne d'Arc* and *Jaureguiberry* lying off the island. When I informed the Admiral that I had some prisoners whom I had been ordered to repatriate, he told me he was going to land and occupy the island, which he proceeded to do forthwith. I thought we would not be out of it, so set off in our steamboat with a Maxim and four dismounted Glasgow Yeomanry – the prisoners' guard. The wretched inhabitants, who were nearly starving, were only too pleased to see us. We first hoisted the French flag on the old castle. Then the Admiral made a speech and appointed Lieut. Trabaud the French Governor of the Lebanon. The latter at once took up his residence on shore, keeping with him fifty French Bluejackets, two guns and two machine-guns: so I called on him and handed over our prisoners. I suggested to my Glasgow yeomen that they should apply to have the word 'Ruad' added to their regimental battle honours when they returned to Scotland! Ruad itself is a curious old place. It dates back to the time of the Phoenicians, and one can still see remains of the ancient walls. It is merely a rock, about 500 by 200 yards, covered with houses: and has a population of about two thousand. All the inhabitants are either sponge-fishers or sailors. On the highest point of the island there

is a fine old castle or fort, very picturesque. The people are entirely
dependent on rain for water, and every house has a large cistern
cut in the rock underneath it. Ruad lies only about a mile from
the mainland, and from this time on we used it as a starting-point
for sending off and receiving spies, who used frequently to swim at
night from the island to the mainland and vice versa.

We sailed in the evening, and during the night ran in close to
the coast. About fifteen miles north of Beirut, we launched a small
native sailing boat – which we had previously captured – with two of
my agents on board, and sent them off with a 'soldier's wind' – wind
blowing the way they were heading. They had their instructions,
and were told that when they had carried these out they were to try
and find their way back somehow to Ruad. I might mention that
they never did so. Whether they were 'wrong-'uns', or whether they
were scuppered by the Turks, I never heard. This, however, was only
one of many such attempts made by us to obtain information as to
what was going on behind the Turkish front line.

The same day we sent off a 'plane, which flew as far as Nazareth
and back. The observer saw nothing of importance, but dropped
letters written by Turkish prisoners of war in Egypt to their
friends, saying how happy and how well treated they were. Mere
propaganda, of course, but at the same time true.

One morning – it was in early September – we received orders
to sail to assist the French blockading squadron in bringing away
about six thousand Armenians who were fighting for their lives
somewhere near Alexandretta. I went on board the *Jeanne d'Arc* and
saw the French Admiral, who confirmed this, and said these people
were being massacred by the Turks and that it was up to us to do
our best for them. So off we pushed. I had with me Herbert, Paul,
and eight of my faithful Glasgow yeomen.

Next day we received a wireless from the French cruiser *Desaix*,
telling us to take off the rearguard of these Armenians, who were
fighting in the Bay of Antioch. We arrived there at daylight, and
brought off three hundred, including two poor old women who
must each have been well over eighty years of age, but had both had

their legs broken. When the first boat reached the shore – the Turks were gaily firing away all the time – it was met by the Armenian Commandant, who was carrying something wrapped up in a cloth, which he asked should be taken to the Admiral. He said that it was a proof that he and his friends were really fighting the Turks. A proof it was – for on opening the parcel we found a Turk's head freshly hacked away from its body.

We got our refugees on board without much incident. As they came up the gangway, I had their arms taken from them – and what a collection these were! Every kind of gun, rifle and revolver that was ever made. Many of them were charged, so I put half a dozen Armenians to unload them. In some cases the only way to do this was to fire them, and, as I thought the Armenians knew more about antiquities than our men did, I gave the former the job. Incidentally, one nearly blew my head off, the bullet touching my hair just above my ear, and the explosion completely deafening me. One man arrived on board in a frock coat, carrying two rifles slung on his back and a Singer's sewing machine. He turned out to be the village tailor. They were all dirty and pretty miserable. They told me that they had been for forty-nine days in the mountain – Gebel Musa – and, running short of ammunition, had just made up their minds to shoot their women and children and to die fighting, when, fortunately for them, we turned up. But they were an ungrateful crowd and had not been on board for four hours before they were complaining about the food. We took them to Port Said, where the whole lot were put into a camp on the Sinai side of the Canal.

8

More Coastal Work

September, 1915–May, 1916

FOR ABOUT THE NEXT eight months we were kept steadily at our old job on the Syrian and Asia Minor coasts. Until October, 1915, we were (considering all things) fairly lucky: but in the first half of that month the wind, as Mr Jarndyce would have said, veered to the east: and from that time on we suffered our fair share of misadventures.

It was Paul and Trouillet who were the first to leave us – not by reason of any intention of their own. On the morning of the 9th October they set out in one of the 'planes to fly to Beersheba. The time passed and they did not return. After they had been away for three hours I was sure that they must have had an accident, and I sent another machine up in search of them. This machine flew the whole way to Beersheba, but although the observer collected useful information about the enemy, Paul's 'plane was not sighted. There was nothing for it but to wait close in to the shore and hope for the best. When I sent any of my men off on a flight I always gave them flares, and instructed them that if they had to make a forced landing they were first to destroy their machines and then to try to make their way to the shore, where if they burnt their flare at night we might have a chance of taking them off. So for the next two nights we kept the *Anne* cruising off that part of the coast; but with no result. We were all very despondent, as both Paul (who had been decorated by the French Admiral with the Croix de Guerre only a few weeks before) and Trouillet had been very popular on board. Moreover, it did not cheer me up to remember that de l'Escaille had often told me that in his opinion a seaplane with floats could not possibly alight on land without crashing badly, and that the chances were that the occupants would be killed.

But there was no good to be got out of hanging on indefinitely in the hopes that our 'missing' would turn up, and on the 13th we sailed for Ruad, whence we had to send a 'plane over Tarsus. We recovered some of our spirits by presenting Trabaud, the Governor, with a flag we had made for him on board. It was a fine flag – with the ancient arms of Ruad (a lion chained to a palm tree) tastefully embroidered. Trabaud was tickled to death. Soon after this we returned to Port Said, where we heard that our people had intercepted a German wireless, saying that one of our 'planes had been brought down, and the aviators captured: so we felt fairly certain that Paul and Trouillet were at least alive.

Later we heard what had happened. It appeared that they had had engine trouble and eventually were forced to come down. The pilot selected the softest-looking spot he could see and made a beautiful landing. Of course, both floats were smashed, but neither the pilot nor observer was flung out of the machine, or in fact injured in any way, which certainly was astounding. They were at once surrounded by Arabs, who seized all their property, including glasses, cigarette-cases, etc. and even some of their clothes were taken off them. They were having rather a bad time of it when some Turkish officers rode up and made the Arabs hand back everything they had taken, mounted Paul and Trouillet on camels and took them into Beersheba. Here they were treated well, and when they found Paul had no money, the Turks gave him thirty Napoleons and a new suit. I was rather amused when I heard about the new suit, as I remembered that on the morning Paul was leaving the ship to go on the flight, he had on what he considered his best uniform, and I was chaffing him about it. Apparently the Turks didn't think much of it either.

About a couple of months later I received from Paul a very cleverly worded letter which, of course, had been censored by the Turks. He wrote it from a prisoners of war camp, and gave me an account of this accident. He said that when the Turkish officers had taken them from the Arabs they mounted them on camels and rode into Beersheba, and that close to the town his camel had shied at some railway trucks and thrown him. As a matter of fact, I knew Paul to be a first-rate man on either a horse or a camel, and doubted if his toss had ever taken place: so, reading between the lines, I came to the conclusion that he was telling us that the enemy's railway had reached Beersheba – the very information that he had been sent on the flight to obtain. He also mentioned that the Turkish officers, including some aviators, had been very kind to him. This also was a way of telling us that the enemy now had aeroplanes on this front.

Months later I was talking to one of our agents and he told me that a café-keeper – a Jew – in Hebron, had said to him that a little time earlier, an English officer had been brought through Hebron as a prisoner, and when passing his shop had asked him for some brandy. Having drunk it, the officer said he was sorry he had no money to pay for it, but that he would give him a paper. So he wrote an IOU, and signed it 'R. Paul'. My man saw the paper, and tried to buy it; but even when offered ten shillings for it the Jew refused, saying, 'No; I know the British officer was a gentleman, and am sure he will pay me himself some day.' In 1920 I saw Paul and told him about this. He said, of course, he was going to pay at the first chance he got.

But this was all afterwards, and in the meantime we lost one of our best agents. He was a Jew, and I landed him at Athlit one night early in November. (Athlit is a small ruined town on a rocky peninsula. As a matter of fact the present native town is built inside the remains of what was once a Crusaders' fortress – almost the last fortress, I believe, that the Crusaders abandoned when they left Palestine.) The landing itself was without incident, and I got back to the *Anne* safely. Our agent too, as it turned out, was safe enough at first. There was a small Jewish colony about two miles inland, for which he was to make, where he was to arrange a regular system not only for obtaining information but also handing it on to us. He did this thoroughly well, but unluckily we were unable to call and pick him up for some little time. The weather was against us, and it was not until the 2nd December that I landed and tried to find him. But it was too late. He had got impatient and, taking another man with him, had tried to get through the Turkish lines to our own. Both of these men were seen and, after putting up a good fight, our agent was killed. His friend, although wounded, reached the English trenches.

But our agent had done one good job before he died. He had instructed some Jews on shore how to signal to us by hanging out, apparently without care, their sheets and blankets. By this means, for example, we learnt that Paul and Trouillet had been taken up country.

About this time our 'planes were troubling us a good deal. Whenever we tried to launch them they had all sorts of minor troubles, such as cylinders burning out, etc. The fact was that the machines were old, and we ought not to have been asked to fly them. De l'Escaille was repeatedly cabling to France for new machines, but without result. I expect the people were far too busy to trouble about us.

By the middle of November the old *Anne*, too, was not up to the mark, and we had to take her to Alexandria to have her cleaned below the water line. She wanted it badly – we could only knock eight knots out of her. Now that submarines were about it was perfectly ridiculous sending 'planes to sea in such a ship. The whole time I was in her we never did more than eleven knots, and that only once. What we wanted was a fast cross-channel-steamer kind of ship capable of something like twenty knots: but *faute de mieux* we carried on in the *Anne*. Nor could I get the barrels I wanted, although I wrote again to Navy House.

Our luck was still out, and on the 22nd December we lost another 'plane. We were off Gaza, and I sent off de Saizeu and Ledger for a flight to Beersheba. They never returned. A fog came up, and for some time I could not send out another 'plane to look for them. When I did, nothing was seen, and after cruising about in case either of our missing men got down to the coast, we returned to Port Said. Just after Christmas we picked up an enemy wireless, saying that our 'plane had landed because of engine trouble and that de Saizeu was a prisoner. Poor Ledger had been shot, as he had foolishly fired at the Turks as they approached.

Towards the end of January, 1916, I was cheered up when, on one of our periodical visits to Port Said, I found my old friend, HMS *Euryalus*, with Admiral Wemyss on board. The latter had come to take over the naval command in that part of the world. One day soon afterwards we received a signal saying that the C-in-C (Admiral Wemyss) wished to see me on board the flagship. When I arrived I was shown into his cabin, where were the captains of all His Majesty's ships – from battleships to trawlers – then in port.

At first I thought some mistake had been made about me (I was the only soldier present), so I tried to make myself as small as possible. The Admiral made a short speech, telling us he had taken over command of the station, and he hoped, etc. etc.: and then he went round the room, shaking hands and having a few words with everybody. It was wonderful how he remembered the people he had met in Gallipoli. 'Hello, so and so!' he would say, 'I think we met last at W Beach in Gallipoli.' But he made one mistake. He shook hands with the Captain of the Port – Port Said – and said, 'V Beach, I think.' 'No, sir,' replied the officer, 'I am the Captain of the Port.' 'Ah! and how is the Port?' asked the Admiral, and passed on. When he came to me he said, 'Hello, Rickmers! how are you?' and had quite a long quack.

This time, on our arrival at Port Said, we found also the *Ben-my-chree*, a seaplane-carrier in command of Lieut.-Commander Malone, and another seaplane-carrier, the *Empress*. We were now formed into a seaplane squadron under the command of Malone. The squadron consisted of the *Ben-my-chree*, the *Empress*, the *Anne* and the *Raven*. The two first of these ships were fast cross-channel steamers with big hangars built on their after-deck, capable of holding six 'planes. They, of course, carried up-to-date powerful machines, so we felt our noses rather out of joint with our poor old French craft. This Malone, by the way, was the man who afterwards became famous as Lieut.-Colonel Malone, of Pelmanism and Bolshevist fame. When I first met him he was only twenty-four years

Left: Lewen Weldon
aboard HMS *Anne*

Below: *Aenne Rickmers* ashore at Mudros, 1915

Left: return of seaplane to mother ship after flight

Above: Damage to *Aenne Rickmers* hold caused by torpedo

Left: Lieutenant R. Gaskell, Captain of *Aenne Rickmers*

Above: HMS *Anne* in Castellorizo harbour

Left: Lieut John Kerr,
Captain of HMS *Anne*

Above: Landing the XXIXth Division at Sudd-el-Bahr, Gallipoli, 25th April 1915
Munsters, Dublins and Hampshires on the foreshore

Left: Young Arab boy
on the Red Sea

Right: one of our 'agents'

HMY *Managem*

Local boatmen who handled the small boats used to land the 'agents'

Left: Commander A. Cain DSC,
Captain of HMY *Managem*

Below: Officers and crew of HMY *Managem*
L to R, sitting: Major Ian Smith, Captain Cain, Captain Weldon,
Lieutenant Reeves, Midshipman Smith, PO Goldie

Captain L. B. Weldon MC
Surveyor-General of Egypt 1920–23

old, clever and shy, but too young to have the command he had. By this time we were very expert at getting away our 'planes. One day, for instance, I remember we only took 1 minute 20 seconds hoisting out a 'plane into the water. The engine started 30 minutes later, and in another half-minute the machine was in the air. So in 5 minutes 20 seconds we had her flying. Not bad work!

I have said that we had our fair share of misadventures, but in one instance, at least, the luck was all on our side. At the beginning of February we put into Ruad, and at the request of the Governor flew over the mainland opposite to see what the enemy was doing there. We spotted nothing, and the next day the sea was too rough to launch a 'plane, so we decided to run to Famagusta and arrange with the Governor to send us a wireless when the weather had moderated and we could return and fly. It was a great stroke of luck that I decided to do this, for some days later we heard that two hours after we left a German submarine turned up and cruised round the island, evidently looking for us, and then chased us over to Cyprus. It had struck me as being silly, lying for days at Ruad within a mile of the Turkish coast. All the enemy had to do was to send a wireless – they had wireless stations ashore – to their submarines informing them we were anchored there. So I was glad our captain agreed with me and pushed off. The submarine missed us, but unfortunately came across the French cruiser *Amiral Charner*, put a torpedo into her and sank her. Out of a crew of about 500 only two men were picked up alive five days later on a raft; there were fourteen dead on it – one a raving lunatic and the other just alive, having kept himself from dying of thirst by cutting his arm and drinking his own blood.

When I next visited Port Said I went on board the *Ben-my-chree* and had a long talk with the Squadron Commander, Malone, with reference to my position now that he and the British 'planes had arrived. I suggested that he should only send the French 'planes in us, as we knew them. He agreed to this, and next day l received orders that I was to consider myself as Intelligence Officer attached to the French seaplanes, and that I was to take my orders from de l'Escaille, which suited me all right.

We sailed again on the 6th March, and as enemy submarines were apparently getting busy in these parts we were given a small French torpedo-boat, No. 250, as an escort. On this voyage we had as observers for the first time three men of the British seaplane squadron, namely Finney, Wedderspoon and Bird, and a new French pilot, Santrey. I had noticed that a lot of the French officers' and ships' names began with 'de', such as de Saizieu, de l'Escaille, Destrem, Desaix, Destres, so I suggested that not to let him feel out of it we should call him 'de Santrey'. However, he didn't seem to appreciate the play on his name, and plain 'Santrey' he was left. The next two days we made successful flights over El Arish, to Libni, Hellal and Kossaima. Some of these flights meant that the 'planes were away overland for two and a half hours, covering a distance of about 120 miles, which was not bad, considering the age of the machines and the low horse-power of the engine – 80 hp only.

When we again returned to Port Said we found things in the squadron were not running smoothly. There was a lot of petty jealousy. The Intelligence Officer in the *Ben-my-chree* was Erskine Childers, the author of *The Riddle of the Sands*. It was just typical of our authorities at home. Here they had a man who, I should have thought, would have been invaluable to them on account of his knowledge of the North Sea, and they had promptly sent him out as an intelligence officer to a ship working on the coasts of Sinai, Syria and Asia Minor. One day rather an amusing thing happened in connection with Childers. He said he wanted to see me, and when I went to his cabin he showed me an album of some excellent photographs taken in Sinai, and said I might like to study them as it would give me some idea of the kind of country we were flying over. I looked them through and praised them greatly. But I didn't tell him that they were my own photographs which I had taken myself when I was out in Sinai with our survey party in 1908.

Looking back on the days when I was connected with the British seaplane squadron, it is interesting to note that it had in it Malone, now, I believe, famous as a Communist; Childers, now a leading Sinn Feiner; and Wedgwood Benn, the well-known Radical

MP. Malone now took over an island in the Canal and rigged up hangars and quarters for his staff on it. Luckily I was left severely alone, and took my orders from the French.

We sailed again on the 15th April with our old friend the French TB 250 as escort. Malone came with us as a passenger to see, I suppose, how we ran things in the *Anne*. He had quite an eventful trip. When off Wadi Gaza we launched a 'plane, but there was too much swell for it to rise from the water and it was hit by a big wave, capsized and sank. We picked up the men all right. In the afternoon we sent away our second 'plane, which made a flight to Shellal and reported a large camp there. We just had this 'plane hoisted on board when we heard a loud explosion in the sea between us and our escort. At first we all thought a submarine must have been spotted by our escort and fired at. But suddenly my little Sudanese orderly – Bakir Ahmed – called out, 'Look, sir!' and pointed skyward. I looked up, and there, right over us, were two enemy aeroplanes. The explosion was caused by a bomb they had dropped on us. They then dropped a couple more, which went wide of us, and continued by opening fire on us with their machine-guns. We replied with rifle fire, but as they were at a height of 2,000 feet, did no good. Neither we nor our escort had any anti-aircraft guns. After about half an hour they retired, and when they were distant some considerable way we elevated our 12-pounder as much as we could and fired a common shell after them. The only damage done to us was that our wireless aerial was shot away. These were the first enemy aircraft seen by us in these parts – later we saw more than enough – so we at once reported their presence by wireless and proceeded to El Arish, where we made a flight next morning, the machine being heavily shelled by the enemy.

We then returned to Port Said, but sailed again the following day after we had coaled and taken on board two 'planes. While in port Malone sent for me and informed me that on our return the French seaplane squadron would be leaving Port Said, and that he would most likely want me to go and work with the British squadron on the island.

On 21st April we made for Castellorizo. This island is situated in a lovely bay quite close to the mainland and has a beautiful little land-locked harbour into which we steamed. We went in bow first and had only just room to turn. The island consists of a rocky mountain, and the town is a cluster of stone-built houses with red-tiled roofs, rising in tiers up the mountain slope from the water's edge. The inhabitants were Greeks who had lived for centuries by piracy. There had once been a few Turks, but when the war broke out the Greeks had driven them out and had hoisted the Greek flag. The French then came along, and as they required the island as a depot on the Asia Minor coast, they hauled down the Greek flag and hoisted their own, installing a French naval officer as Governor and leaving a garrison of Bluejackets, who set to work to mount guns and fortify the island in case some Turks attacked it. A boom was placed across the mouth of the little harbour.

I landed and called on the Governor. He explained that he wanted us to do a flight from there to Makry and Tersana, further west along the coast, and then from the latter place to Marmarice, as he had received a report that a German submarine was making its base near there and had a depot of petrol somewhere handy. The idea was to keep the ship concealed in Castellorizo and pay surprise visits to these places by 'plane. All the French officers were very pleasant, and went out of their way to give us a good time. Tersana, to which it was proposed to fly, was an island in the Gulf of Makry inhabited by Greeks, whose chief was a regular old pirate with whom the French were on good terms. All this having been arranged, we sent off some mechanics and stores to Tersana in the French trawler *Nord Caper*. They were safely landed there under cover of darkness and sat down to await the arrival of the 'plane that was to fly from Castellorizo over Makry, next morning. At 6 a.m. on the 22nd April we sent off the 'plane on its long flight with Lieut. Smith, HLI, as observer, and Lieut. Wright, RNAS, as pilot. While they were away the chief engineer, Bishop, and I went ashore and climbed up the mountain at the back of the town. It was a thousand-feet climb up a winding stone-hewn stairway, but well worth the trouble. We had a glorious view from the top, and I took several photographs which turned out well. In the afternoon we were shown all the sights of the town by a French lieutenant, Micheller by name. There was a fine old castle, supposed to have been built by the Knights of St John before they settled in Rhodes. We also were shown a lovely ancient Greek rock tomb. Some of the masonry in the town dates back to 300 BC, and traces of Roman occupation are also found there.

We were rather anxious next morning as the 'plane had not returned, till the *Nord Caper* came in and informed us that it was safe at Tersana, where it had come down for some petrol. The next day we got a wireless from the trawler telling us that the 'plane was carrying out a flight from Tersana to Marmarice, and she turned up safely alongside the *Anne* at 7 p.m., having had a very interesting flight. There was no doubt about the employment of Makry as a submarine base. When the 'plane got there there was a lot of oil on the surface of the sea, and the submarine could only just have left. How we did curse that we had not arrived a few hours earlier, when we might have caught her!

On the 25th April I went on shore and saw the Governor, who asked me if we would give a passage to forty-five Turkish prisoners and their officer, which I agreed to do. It was the anniversary of the Gallipoli landing, and I spent the morning taking photographs of the inhabitants, who were rigged out like prize rabbits in all their native finery, this being their Easter.

In the afternoon we embarked the prisoners. Amongst them was a Turkish *yusbashi* (captain), a nice old boy about fifty-two, and a *cadi* (judge). I gave the two of them a cabin to themselves and put all the rest in the hold. At first the *yusbashi* and the *cadi* were very nervous – they didn't know how we were going to treat them – but after a bit I found they knew a little Arabic, so I yapped to them and put them more or less at ease. Every day on our way to Port Said I played 'tric-trac' (backgammon) with the *yusbashi* and split a bottle of beer. The consequence was that he went out of his way to see that his own men, the rank and file, behaved themselves.

This *yusbashi* was the proud possessor of four medals: one long service, one Turko-Grecian War, one Yemen, and one Turkish life-saving decoration. He explained carefully to me that he had three for taking life and one for saving life, and I think he was proudest of the last. I suppose it would be the least common among the Turks (and, after all, among most nations in these days).

We sailed on the 25th April in the evening, and arrived safely at Port Said on the 26th. We disembarked our 'planes and handed over our prisoners. The *yusbashi* and the *cadi* took an affectionate farewell of me, and the former said that when the war was over I was to come and stay with him in Constantinople, and he would show me round and give me plenty of riding and shooting. I heard later that the poor old boy had been sent to France, and have often wondered how he fared. But I may mention that when I landed the prisoners there was an armed guard to meet them and to escort them to the station. They were being taken to Ismaila. I thought it was rather bad luck on the *yusbashi* and the *cadi* to be marched through the crowded street to be stared at. So, having told the lieutenant of the guard that I would be responsible for them, I put the two into a cab and drove them to the station. They were exceedingly grateful, as it would have been very trying for them otherwise.

Just after this a tragedy occurred on board. For the last three months we had had with us a bull-terrier named 'Major', the property of the skipper. One day, when the poor brute was running round the deck, he slipped and fell overboard. He would have been all right if he had fallen in the water, but unluckily he hit his head on the last step of the gangway. He managed, however, to walk all the way up to the bridge, where he lay down, licked my hand – and died. He had burst his lungs. There was not a man on board who was not upset at losing him. He had been a great favourite with us all.

The next few days we were very busy shipping the French squadron 'planes – which had been taken to pieces and packed in cases – and stores. The French flying officer and I went off to a farewell dinner given by the British Flying Squadron. At the end of the dinner rather a funny encounter occurred. One of the young British pilots – without at all meaning to be rude – turned to the Frenchman, Destrem, and said, 'How is it that all you French pilots are such old men?' 'Ah!' said Destrem, as quick as lightning, looking up and down the table at all the British boys, 'we do not rob the nurseries.' As a matter of fact, in spite of his beard and stoutness, Destrem was only thirty-three years old; but our *men* were boys.

Late in the evening of the 3rd May, when all the personnel of the French squadron had come on board, and after Malone had said farewell, we sailed. I had been specially asked by Malone to go with them, and I was only too pleased to do so. We made for Malta, and had instructions on arrival there to transfer the Frenchmen to a French seaplane-carrier that would meet us.

We had with us as escort the French torpedo-boat destroyer *Haché*. On the 6th May we sighted Crete and kept to the northward. During the night we were nearly run down by some big ship. It was really surprising how few collisions were heard of in those days, considering that no lights were ever carried. I suppose the reason was that everyone kept an extra good look out. This part of the sea was well patrolled by sweepers, trawlers and destroyers. We sighted Malta on the 9th May, and arrived off Valletta Harbour about 9 a.m. We then had to wait till the gunboat HMS *Hasard* came to show us the way through the minefield. These mines were supposed to have been laid for the enemy by a Greek schooner – nice people the Greeks! – and just before we arrived the battleship *Russell* had run into one sunk. Next day the *Erin*, formerly Sir Thomas Lipton's yacht, was sunk by one also, so we had cause to congratulate ourselves on our safe arrival. We began to transfer our Frenchmen to their new ship, the *Compenas*. They didn't appreciate the change a bit, and said she was not nearly as comfortable as the *Anne*. They had received orders to sail for Cephalonia as soon as they were ready. We presented de l'Escaille with a large silver cigarette-box with the French and British flying badges engraved on it, and he was most awfully pleased. On the 12th May we took an affectionate farewell of our good friends the French. As their ship passed the *Anne*, all our crew turned out and gave them three cheers, to which they responded. We were very sorry to part with them, and I never wish to meet a nicer or more gallant lot of men. Whenever one of our French flying men was asked if he could make such and such a flight, sometimes almost impossible, and at any rate most dangerous, his reply, without a moment's hesitation, was always the same, '*Je peux assayer.*'

During the period that HMS *Anne* acted as carrier to the French seaplane squadron one hundred and eighteen flights were made from her. The actual hoisting of the seaplanes overboard and inboard was carried out without a single one being damaged, which reflects great credit on Captains Gaskell and Kerr, and also the 1st Officer, Lieut. Buck. Two 'planes only were captured by the enemy and only one life lost, a very fine record considering the low horse-power of the 'planes and the long flights they accomplished from the ship overland to such places as Beersheba, Kossauna, Ludd, Adana, Tarsus, Samaria, Nazareth, Osmanie, and many others.

9

Various Cruises

May–August, 1916

OUR SHORT STAY in Malta had one useful result, for while we were there the mounting of our 12-pounder was altered so that the gun could be elevated and used against aircraft. We felt much happier when this was done. No one likes to be unable to hit back.

On our way back to Port Said we received another reminder that enemy submarines were getting busily to work in our part of the world. It was when we were off Crete, and we were suddenly ordered to alter our course for the island of Milo. Arriving there, we found we had to wait in the harbour as the authorities had information that there was a German submarine in the neighbourhood. As a matter of fact a small steamer of about 500 tons – the *Clifford* – was sunk by this submarine the next day.

Milo is a very hilly little island, containing a few scattered villages and a fine harbour. How the allies had been allowed to occupy it I don't know, as in reality it belonged to Greece. It often struck me in those days that both we and the French were remarkably handy at mopping up little bits of Grecian territory. But no one seemed to object, and the islands were certainly very useful as places of refuge.

We only stayed a night at Milo, and arrived at Port Said in the evening of the 21st May. Apparently we had been lucky, as on the day before four German aeroplanes had flown over the town and dropped twelve bombs, killing two Europeans and four natives and wounding sixteen.

While we had been away there had been a change in the command. Malone had gone home and Commander Samson had taken over from him. Samson and his many gallant deeds are too well known for me to say anything about him or them, but what I noticed particularly was that, whenever there was some extra dangerous flight to be made, or perhaps an extra heavy sea running in which there was a good chance of the 'plane being smashed after being hoisted out from the ship, the OC himself invariably went as pilot, instead of sending one of his officers, which really he should have done.

Next day I went on board the *Ben-my-chree* and reported myself to the latter. I asked him if, now that my Frenchmen had gone, I was to return to the military. 'Certainly not,' he said, and added that he understood the *Anne* could not do without me, finishing up by telling me that I was to carry on exactly as before. In fact, he was extremely nice, and I felt quite pleased. In the next few days we heard conflicting rumours of the battle of Jutland. The first news was that we had lost twelve ships, the next that the Germans had lost fifty. It was difficult to know what to believe: but when on the 8th June we received the news of the loss of Lord Kitchener, we could not feel very cheerful. At this time the Military Intelligence Officer, Port Said, was a Captain Woolley; and as he had gone to Cyprus for a few days, I used to fill in my time by going to his office and keeping things running for him. But on the 15th June we received orders to steam through the Canal to Suez, where we were to ship ammunition for the Hejaz.

We reached Suez Roads on the next day, and found the *Scotia* and the monitor *Humber* there. On the 19th we moved into the inner harbour and took on board tons of barley, rice, coffee, etc. Colonel Clayton arrived with Captain Cornwallis and Sayad Bey Ali. The latter was a Kaimakam of Artillery in the Egyptian Army and was going with us to Port Sudan to take command of two Gippy mountain batteries that we were going to ship and take over to Jeddah, where they were to join the King of the Hejaz's Army. The Kaimakam wasn't a bit keen on the job, and explained to me that he had plenty of medals and a nice comfortable office with a telephone in the War Office in Cairo, and that the last thing he wanted to do was to go and fight in the Gebal (desert). He was quite emotional when speaking about this; although, as a matter of fact, he did extremely well later on.

On the evening of the 22nd June, having shipped a few stores and rifles and £30,000 in gold, we sailed for Port Sudan with Cornwallis and the Bey on board. Speaking of this gold reminds me of a rather amusing story; for the truth of which, however, I cannot vouch. A certain ship – I won't mention her name – took on board some boxes of sovereigns (about £5,000 in each box), which were to be taken to Jeddah and there handed over to a representative of the Cherif. At Jeddah the representative came on board all right, took delivery, gave a receipt and departed. Shortly after he had gone the officer in whose charge the gold had been, discovered that one box had been left behind apparently by mistake. Of course, he went ashore, and after a great deal of trouble found the Cherif 's representative and explained matters to him. When the latter heard of the one box which was still lying on the ship he simply nodded, and said 'maloum' (of course). It then dawned on the officer that this box had been left as 'baksheesh' for the trouble that had been taken in bringing the money from Egypt.

To get back to my story. The Red Sea in June is no place for a white man, and we were properly baked. I had all my hair taken off with clippers; our uniforms merely consisted of a pair of shorts and a vest. We arrived at Port Sudan at noon on the 26th June and went alongside the quay. It is a very up-to-date little harbour with big hydraulic cranes along the quay, and there is an excellent hotel run by the Sudan Government Railways. In the afternoon we began to take on board the two batteries of artillery and 150 mules. The Sirdar, Sir Reginald Wingate, came down and inspected the troops, and presented the Bey with a walking-stick – to buck him up, I presume. The heat there was something appalling. The only place we could put the mules was on the foredeck, where they had a pretty warm time standing on iron decks with no awnings over them, and the thermometer registering about 120° in the shade – when you could find any shade, that is to say. Colonel Pearson, who was going to Jeddah as an intelligence officer, came on board; and we sailed on the evening of the 27th, arriving off Jeddah next day. The town had just been captured by the Cherif of Mecca (later known as the King of the Hejaz), aided by our aeroplanes flying from the *Ben-my-chree*. The Turkish OC had quickly surrendered with all his troops (about 1,600) and six German officers. Of the latter the Arabs killed four before our people could stop them – Germans weren't popular even in those parts!

One of the sons of the Cherif called for Said Bey Ali and took him ashore; and the next day we began to unship our batteries, hositing the mules in slings over the side down into dhows. We had got half away when we got an order to keep one battery on board and proceed with it up the coast to a place called Rabigh, where it was to be landed. So off we sailed, and arrived at Rabigh next morning. There was a fairly large natural harbour there, but no town, the nearest village being some kilometres inland. Immediately we were in the harbour we were surrounded by dhows; but these soon cleared off, their occupants refusing to land the battery, and saying that all they wanted was food and ammunition. They were a wild-looking lot. HMS *Hardinge* was there with us, and Captain Linberry went off in a boat to the shore to see what he could do; but the Arabs took up their rifles and threatened to shoot him if he put his foot on land. Nice sort of allies they were! He had to return, and we sent a wireless to Jeddah explaining the situation and asking for instructions. We received a reply, saying we were to await the arrival of the *Surada*, a BI transport – with a local Sheikh Nassir on board who would arrange matters. Linberry was naturally annoyed and sent his interpreter, a native, on shore to try and persuade the Arabs to let us land the mules, but Hussein – the Cherif's son – who was in command of the Arabs, refused, and also refused to come on board and talk things over. At this period of the war the Arabs were very suspicious of us, and were not out to take any risks; of course, they changed later on.

The *Surada* arrived in the morning, having on board the other battery that we had landed at Jeddah, Colonel Pearson and Sheikh

Nassir. We all met in the *Hardinge* and discussed the situation. Sheikh Nassir had been ashore and seen Sheikh Hussein, and said that dhows would be sent during the morning to unload grain, rifles and ammunition, but that the Arabs did not want the artillery. So we agreed not to land anything till we had communicated with our people at Jeddah – and this we did by wireless. Later, we received an order to return to Jeddah, and did so gladly.

We got back to Jeddah on the 3rd July, when dhows came alongside and we were able to send away our artillery – greatly pleased we were to get rid of it, too – and, to give the ship a thorough washing down. We had had these batteries with us for six days, and when they first came we were told it would only be for twelve hours.

Next day fifty men of the Warwickshire Regiment were brought to us for a passage to Port Sudan. They had been brought over to act as escort to 1,400 Turkish prisoners whom it was intended to send to Egypt; but that fell through, as the Arabs refused to hand them over. Next day, however, we received an order to send the fifty soldiers over to the *Dufferin*, which was lying not far away. We were now having a bad time, as we had no ice and were running short of everything, and it wasn't pleasant to be drinking hot water. The next few days we were busy unloading our barley, etc. We heard that our late passengers, the artillery, had been in action at Mecca and had done very well. They knocked down the only Turkish fort that was holding. So the Arabs had become quite pleased with them. To fill in the time we used to drop lines over the side of the ship, and we caught some extraordinary fish all colours of the rainbow. The bag one day included a shark – there were plenty of them about. At last, on 7th July, having finished unloading and having collected mails for home from all the other ships, we sailed for Suez, where we arrived on the 11th July.

As the *Anne* was to be docked, I managed to get a few days' leave; and immediately after these were finished I was pushed off to Alexandria with Kerr, our captain, to see if we could find a ship suitable for seaplane-carrying there. After looking round for some time, we actually found an ex-Austrian Lloyd, a prize, about 8,000 tons and with a speed of 18 knots. We knew at once that she would suit, so we returned to Port Said and reported. Naturally we were pleased with ourselves, but as soon as negotiations were started, the Prize Court stepped in and refused to part with the ship. So we had to stick to the old *Anne* after all. On the 1st August I returned to Suez, and a day or two later the *Anne* steamed through the Canal to Port Said. Once more we were back on our old hunting-ground – or, rather, hunting-seas – and it was not long before our 'planes were flying over Gaza and Beersheba again. But it was not until a week later that we were sent on a job that is worth talking about. Then we did take part in something a little out of the ordinary.

On the morning of the 6th August, Commander Samson sent for me and told me we were to rendezvous with the French Admiral, who was going to bombard Mersina, on the Asia Minor coast. He gave me the French Admiral's orders and plans of attack to study, and we sailed the same evening, with a French destroyer, the *Voltigeur*, as escort. At about 4 o'clock on the morning of the 10th August we reached a position about five miles east of Mersina town, where we were met by the French flagship, the *Pothau*, which was accompanied by some destroyers and trawlers. At 6 a.m. the *Pothau* steamed in nearer the town and anchored about two miles from the shore. We lay to five hundred metres astern of her, while three destroyers and five trawlers kept circling round us in case a submarine appeared.

Mersina town is a fine-looking place, with several factories and barracks and a railway station, and quite a decent-looking seaport. Although it was early, a good many people came out on the front and watched us. At about 6 a.m. the *Pothau* opened fire on the large barracks south-west of the town, and very soon destroyed them. In the meanwhile we had hoisted out a machine, with Dacre as pilot and Stewart as observer, to bomb enemy craft – a tug-boat and schooners – in the Tarsus Chai, and to look out for submarines. The 'plane returned to the *Anne* after about an hour, having expended all its bombs. The *Pothau*, having destroyed the barracks, next turned her guns on to a large factory which, it had been reported, was used for the manufacture of munitions. This she soon destroyed. She also fired at and partially wrecked the railway station.

When we were keeping up this bombardment every care was taken to avoid destroying private houses, and only one shot went astray. Instead of keeping indoors and in their cellars, as one might have expected them to do, the people in the town actually crowded to the sea front and sat down to watch the ships' fire. We might have been putting up the show just for their benefit by the way they behaved.

Firing ceased about half-past eight and we hoisted out a plane to look at the damage. Later on the *Pothau* sent over a few more shots and destroyed another factory, while another of our 'planes landed a bomb on the railway station. In the meanwhile a Turkish biplane was sighted overhead. It dropped four bombs fairly close to us. We were the only ship that fired at it and were quite pleased with ourselves when, after two of our shells had burst near, it flew away. Apparently it never spotted the 'plane we had up.

We had now accomplished all that we had come for, so the Admiral signalled, thanking us for our assistance and giving us leave to return to Port Said, where we arrived two days later. When I reported to Samson he was much pleased with the satisfactory way everything had gone. Whilst in Port we heard that when the *Raven* and Monitor No. 21 were off el Mada'an, a German aeroplane flew over them and dropped two 100-lb bombs, which fell very close to the monitor. What with submarines and aeroplanes, things were beginning to 'hot up' in these parts!

We sailed again on the 24th August with the French torpedo-boat destroyer *Haché* as escort. We rendezvoused off the Bay of Acre next morning with the *Raven* and *Ben-my-chree*. The latter was not up to time, and we heard later she had run ashore near Athlit in a thick morning mist. Luckily enough she was going slow, did herself no damage, and got off under her own steam. We all hoisted out our 'planes, ten of them altogether, which flew to el Afuleh, where they bombed and destroyed the railway station. On the way back one of the 'planes dropped a bomb at a train and hit the engine – a good shot. It was a pretty fine sight, all the ten 'planes in the air at the same time.

We then steamed down the coast: and when off the ancient town of Askelon sent away our two machines, which flew in and bombed the viaduct over Wady Hesy. Six more machines flew from the other ships, and all returned safely with the exception of one, a Bristol, the pilot of which was Dacre. We cruised all night off the coast, but saw no signs of him. He was our best pilot and the best of good fellows, and he had been among the first Britishers to fly in a seaplane – in fact, he flew before Samson did. We heard some time later that he had been forced to land through engine trouble and had managed to do so with nothing worse than a severe shaking and subsequent capture.

The next day we brought off successfully two flights: over Nablus and Tul el Keram, bombing the latter place; and over Ramleh and Ludd, bombing the large camps there. We then returned to Port Said, arriving there on the morning of the 27th August.

As soon as I went on shore I heard that Woolley had been lost. He had gone to the Gulf of Alexandretta in the *Zaida* – a yacht formerly the property of Lord Rosebery – had struck a mine, and lost twelve men. The survivors had been picked up and taken prisoner by the Turks. I was sorry for him but at the same time I felt that he was looking for it. For some time previously he had been making an elaborate plan to mislead the Turks into thinking that we meant to land a large force in Alexandretta Bay. To this end he had plastered the country in Cyprus with notices such as 'This way to the camp,' 'This way to the aerodrome,' 'Speed of army lorries not to exceed 8 miles an hour,' 'Gun park,' etc., and had asked all of us to tell people here and there, in confidence, that we were going to use Cyprus as a jumping-off ground for Alexandretta. The idea was that the Turks would bring back some of their troops from the Sinai and Mesopotamian front to oppose our landing. Of course, very naturally the Turks mined Alexandretta Bay, and when Woolley, unfortunately, went there in the yacht to see what they were doing, he promptly found out by being blown up.

10

With the Hejaz

August–October, 1916

IN THE 31ST AUGUST, 1916, while we were lying quietly in Port Said, we heard that the *Raven* was to sail with 'planes for the Red Sea. Undoubtedly that was the plan, but circumstances forced it to be altered. For the next morning, just after we had finished breakfast, three Hun aeroplanes flew over the harbour and dropped twelve bombs. We were lying about thirty yards from the *Raven* at the time and had our hatches off unloading bombs. I was on the bridge with the chief engineer watching the 'planes and the effects of our gun-fire, when suddenly a bomb hit the water and burst seven yards off our counter. A few minutes later another whizzed down and burst on the fore deck of the *Raven*, making a big hole in the deck and laying out twelve of her native crew who were sitting there. Yet another burst in a coal dump on the far side of the Canal, sending up a dense black cloud.

Of course, this flying business of the Huns altered matters considerably. The *Raven* was out of action, and so we were not surprised when orders came through that we were to take over her job. In fact, we were quite ready, and sailed the same evening, taking with us Commander Malone, who had returned to Port Said and, as Samson was his senior, had been put in charge of the seaplane depot on the Island, instead of returning to the *Ben-my-chree*.

On our way down the Gulf of Suez we called in at Abu Zenemeh, where a company of Sikhs and two British officers were quartered. Here we sent up a 'plane to see if the Turks were moving from Nekhl to attack our front: but there were no signs of the enemy at all, so we sailed on southward. We had a following wind and it was most uncomfortably hot and damp. The Red Sea is an appalling place in the beginning of September.

At Ras el Maluk we rendezvoused with HMS *Fox* and HMS *Dufferin*. Here, on shore, were about 8,000 Arabs who had just come in to join the Cherif 's army. They were a most motley collection and had arms of every description. We – the British –were now supplying the Cherif 's people with arms, with which we hoped they would make themselves unpleasant to the Turkish garrisons scattered throughout Arabia. But after a while we found that it was a case of giving with one hand and taking away with the other. In other words, certain of the Cherif 's people – I apologise, army – had been struck with a brilliant idea. Having obtained arms gratis and for nothing, why should they not make a good honest profit out of them? And this many of them began doing at once. They shipped the rifles, etc., provided by the benevolent British Government, over to the Egyptian side of the Red Sea and there sold them to the Bedouin. For a time the trade was brisk and lucrative, but soon a service was organised to save us from our friends. To put it differently, we found it necessary to search 'friendly' dhows to see that they were not running arms. So the business languished.

At Ras el Maluk we sent up a 'plane for a show flight, which duly impressed the Arabs, and then for a few days we practised our observers with the wireless which had recently been fitted to our machines. Then on 8th September we sailed again, and anchored off Sherm Rabigh the same evening.

Arabs came off to the ship in small dugout canoes and sold us fish, shells, sponges, etc. The next day we did a flight over all the adjacent villages – the inhabitants being our allies, we only flew to impress them with the value of the machines. We then received orders to proceed to Sherm Yembo. The charts of this coast were very inaccurate and we ran on to a coral reef while feeling our way into the little harbour. But as we were going dead slow we did ourselves no harm, and when the tide came in we reversed our engines and slid off easily. We had some glorious bathing here, but all the time one had to keep a look out for sharks.

On the following morning we weighed anchor and steamed to Yambo town close by. This town is the port for Medina. It is a very quaint old place surrounded with a wall. We were not allowed to land, but several of the inhabitants came off to the ship. At noon we received orders to sail for Hassani Island, where we, together with the *Hardinge* and *Fox*, arrived at daybreak. This island lies nine miles off the coast, and people came to it from the mainland during the hot weather, much in the same way that people go to the seaside from London. Its attractions, however, were limited – in fact, nil. I went on shore with Malone to report if it would be a possible place on which to fit up an aerodrome, whence aeroplanes – or seaplanes – could patrol the coast. We found that it would be quite suitable. We then practised a landing from boats of about 100 Cherifian troops. It was rather comic, and all concerned enjoyed themselves.

We sailed in the evening and ran to the island of Marduna, and hoisted out a 'plane on arrival to 'spot' for the *Fox* and *Hardinge*, who were bombarding Wejj. Later on we sent away a second 'plane, which flew over the enemy's trenches, and reported them deserted. On receiving a signal from the *Hardinge* to say that 100 Turks were entrenched at Sherm Mandarib, about ten miles from our position, we sent up a machine at sunset to see what was doing. This machine returned just as it got dark, and the observer reported that he had seen nothing of the enemy. Next morning, the 14th September, we sent away a 'plane which, having flown over Wejj and its neighbourhood returned and reported the town deserted, but that it had bombed a fort some six miles inland. The *Fox*, however, kept up the bombardment of Wejj for most of the morning.

The next few days we spent in making various flights over Wejj, Monaiber, etc., reporting the presence – or otherwise – of enemy's troops. We used to stand out to sea for the night and come into the mainland in the mornings.

On the 16th September, as we were running out of provisions, etc., we got orders to transfer one of our seaplanes to the *Northbrook*, an Indian marine ship, and to proceed to Suez. As the *Northbrook* had not arrived, we anchored off Hassani Island to wait for her: and there, to pass the time, we fished. Our bag was 200 lb of fish of all sorts – not bad. The next day the *Northbrook* arrived and, having transferred a 'plane to her, we sailed for Suez. We had a fairly rough run and arrived at Suez, where Malone left us, in the afternoon of the 20th. Here we got the news that while one of our 'planes from the *Ben-my-chree* was flying over el Arish it caught fire at a height of about 4,000 feet. Bankes-Price, the pilot, jumped out. His body was picked up out of the sea, with every bone in it broken.

On the 23rd September, having finished coaling re-provisioning the ship, we sailed again for the Red Sea. We arrived at Rabigh on the 26th and found there the cruisers *Espiéglé* and *Dufferin*. After a couple of days the *Hardinge* also turned up. She had Admiral Sir R. Wemyss, Ronald Storrs and Colonel Parker on board – the last named was formerly Governor Sinai.

On the 30th we made a flight with a 'Short' over Ras Masturah, and returned again to Rabigh. Here we took on board a Major Bannatyne, of the 14th Hussars and RAF. His experiences were most interesting, as he had been with General Kelly's column when it was operating against Ali Dinar in Darfur, and he was one of the first men to fly a machine in Central Africa. He was a very good fellow, and I discovered that I knew all his people in Limerick. A couple of years later he was killed while flying in England, his machine catching fire. He came with us and inspected an island north of Rabigh, with the idea that it might be possible to establish an aerodrome on it. I went ashore with him and acted as interpreter. We came to the conclusion that it was unsuitable, and so returned to Rabigh and reported.

The next few days we lay quietly in Rabigh, and spent the time bathing and fishing.

The Arab troops on shore were perpetually letting off their rifles, either by accident or out of sheer devilment. The ship was hit several times, and we were very lucky to have no one injured. I lunched and dined several times on board the *Fox* and *Hardinge*.

The crews of these ships were kept busy building a small pier to facilitate the landing of stores for the Cherif's army.

About this time things seemed to be in a fair muddle here (the Hejaz). There appeared to be no one man in charge. A ship actually arrived from Suez with aeroplanes on board, only to be told that she could go back as there was nowhere to land the 'planes. Our allies, the Arabs, were most suspicious and would not dream of allowing an aerodrome to be built on shore. The senior military officer wanted to keep us there with the seaplanes, but this idea was also unsatisfactory, as every now and then we should have had to run to Suez or Port Sudan for coal and provisions. Yet not only had the aeroplanes to be returned to whence they came, but also 300 British soldiers, for, of course, the Arabs would not consent to their being landed. The latter imagined that once the British had got into the country they would never leave. One would have thought that in these days of wireless telegraphy the authorities in Egypt could have found out all this before sending off the 'planes and men. Still, this had nothing to do with me.

One day I went ashore with Parker Bey to take photos. We had to don Arab headgear.

That same evening a canoe came alongside carrying two of the Cherif's officers. I took them on board into the saloon and found that one was the C-in-C of the Arab army, Aziz Bey Ali, and that the second was his ADC.

Aziz Bey was very interesting. He had formerly been in the Turkish Army and was Enver Pasha's right-hand man during the Turko-Italian war in Tripoli. At the end of that campaign he accompanied Enver to Constantinople where he fell out with the latter, who was jealous of him. So Enver imprisoned him and was going to have him hanged, but the British and French ambassadors intervened, saved him, and sent him to Egypt. In consequence, when we declared war on Turkey, he volunteered to fight for us in order to get a little of his own back on Enver– so here he was.

The ADC was a well-educated young Arab who had fought against us in Mesopotamia, had been taken prisoner, and, after spending a year in a POW camp in India, had volunteered for service with the Cherif's army and had been set at liberty.

I offered Aziz Bey a drink, and he said he would like a whisky and soda. For fun I questioned, 'Scotch or Irish?' To my astonishment he replied eagerly, 'Have you Irish? I prefer it.' After we had provided them with some boxes of cigarettes, for which they had really come, we sent them ashore in one of our cutters.

One evening, as I was standing on the bridge, a couple of bullets whizzed by close to my ear, and I heard a couple of bangs on shore, followed immediately by loud shouts for a boat. We sent a cutter, and brought off an Arab who had a message for me. I asked him why we had been fired at, and he replied simply that the shots had only been intended to attract our attention. Nice people, the Arabs!

With the exception of a trip to Port Sudan, where we arrived just in time for me to celebrate my birthday on shore, we were kept lying more or less idle at Rabigh for several weeks. But on the 26th October the *Raven* came down to relieve us, and we made for Suez, which we reached on the 30th. The next morning I almost wished we had stayed at sea a day or so longer, for a German aeroplane came over and dropped nine bombs on Port Tewfiq. I was on shore driving in an arabeyeh (a cab) at the time, and, trying to be cheerful, I suggested to the driver that he had better put the hood up to make me safer. With perfect gravity he pulled up his horse and did so. I believe he quite thought a bit of leather would keep off a 100 lb bomb.

11

Last Cruises of the Anne

November, 1916–February, 1917

B Y THIS TIME we were becoming quite used to working from either entrance of the Canal, and we knew every landmark between Suez and Port Said, as a London taxi driver knows every shop in Regent Street. It was no surprise to us, therefore, to receive orders for the northern port once again, and we plodded off without delay.

Having arrived at our destination we found that we should not be wanted immediately, so all of us settled down for a few days' peace. At this time Port Said town was crowded with stranded passengers from the P&O ship *Arabia* which had recently been torpedoed. I gathered that she had taken about an hour and a half to sink, and that although two Austrian submarines had stayed on the surface close by, the *City of Marseilles* had gallantly stood by and had taken on board all the passengers. To do them justice, the submarines had not attempted to interfere – it was easy to guess they were not Germans.

I am tempted to say nothing of the next job that fell to our lot. There was certainly nothing romantic about it. In fact we were simply turned into a collier and were sent off with our holds crammed with coal to Cyprus. But the unloading was interesting in a way. The 'coalies' were a mixture of Greek men and girls; and, watching them, it was not difficult to see which were the best workers. Until then I had been unfortunate in my dealings with Greeks, but I took off my hat to those Greek women.

At the beginning of December we were back in Port Said, and not long afterwards I was given the first hint of what was in store for me. One day Captain Ian Smith, the Military Intelligence Officer, came to see us on board the *Anne*. After a bit of a 'yap' he asked me casually if I knew of any yacht suitable for spy work on the Syrian coast. I did not. Then he suggested that if a yacht were found I might like to take charge of the agent- landing-and-collecting business. As I wanted a change I said that I would certainly consider the matter, but I pointed out that permission for me to leave the *Anne* would have to be obtained from the Admiral. Smith thought that this could be arranged, and without saying anything more of the matter went off. A few weeks later I tackled Commander Samson about the job. He was very friendly about it, and said that he would be sorry to lose me but that, if I wanted to go, he would put no obstacles in my way. It was, however, a couple of months before I heard anything definite.

Christmas found us still at Port Said.

I spent Christmas Day on the ship. At the men's dinner-time the Captain and I went round the mess decks, which had been decorated with flags and palms. At each mess the men presented us with half a tumblerful of whisky in which we had to drink their healths and wish them a merry Christmas. *We* felt quite 'merry' by the time we finished the rounds! It was a bit of an ordeal. We lent the men the piano from the saloon and they had a singsong in the afternoon. In the evening we had several guests to dinner, and the day closed without any 'regrettable incidents'.

On the 29th December I received an official order from Samson to the effect that I was to lecture on board the *Ben-my-chree* to all the officers and men of the seaplane squadron on 'Sinai and Syria: the countries and people'. I went off and told him I had never given a lecture in my life; but all the satisfaction I got out of him was, 'Well, you're going to now. What's your cocktail?' On the evening of the 31st I dined with him in the *Ben-my-chree*, and after dinner stepped out on deck to give my lecture. The deck was crammed, Samson and all the senior officers, including Wedgwood Benn (MP), occupying the stalls. I got under weigh, however, and actually, I believe, spoke for an hour. I landed one back at Samson when I was speaking about

Gaza by saying, 'This was where Samson pulled down the pillars of the temple – not your Samson, but Delilah's.' (Loud cheers and whistles.) 'Delilah's Samson did not believe in high explosives,' etc. Amongst other things I mentioned was that in my humble opinion the only three men who ever really knew Sinai and how to 'trek' across it were Moses, Napoleon, and Parker Bey, late Governor of Sinai. Apparently the lecture went off all right.

At the beginning of January we put out to sea once more, but ran into such bad weather that we had to return without having done anything. One of the com 'planes was damaged by the sea and wind.

Enemy submarines were now hard at it in the Mediterranean. On the 3rd January a large Russian cruiser was torpedoed only about six miles out from Port Said. The moment she was struck she began letting off her guns in every direction, which made things too lively to be comfortable for the trawlers and motor launches which hurried to her aid. Nevertheless, 750 of the crew were saved. Only about forty or fifty were lost.

While we were in port the Military Intelligence people informed me that they had procured a yacht – the *Managem* – for the spy business, so I felt pretty sure that my days with the old *Anne* were numbered.

On the 10th January we heard that the *Ben-my-chree* had been sunk by gunfire while in the harbour of Castelorizo. She had gone up there with 'planes to try and locate some 6-inch Turkish guns, which we knew had been placed in position on the mainland opposite. She sailed in company with the French Admiral, who was on his yacht. They went into the little harbour and anchored, intending to land stores and to fly their 'planes from there. It was like sitting in the bull's-eye of a target. The Turks opened fire, and the ninth shot hit the ship and set her on fire. All that could be done was to open the sea-cocks and abandon the vessel. This the crew did, and all got ashore safely, only two men being wounded. All the men behaved well, and Captain Wedgwood Benn got a DSO for his gallant conduct during this unhappy affair. A French destroyer which was also in the harbour got up her anchor and escaped to sea. The crew of the *Ben-my-chree* had to camp out on the mountainside, and later on were taken off the island by French trawlers and brought back to Port Said.

On January 11th we received an order to get our 'planes on board and to proceed to the Red Sea. So, starting work again, we sailed the same evening. We arrived at Suez, where we remained three days awaiting orders. At last we were ordered to proceed to Sherm Hanab on the Arabian coast, south of Wejj. We sailed, and, a couple of days later, rendezvoused with the *Espieglé* and proceeded to Dhaba, whence we made a flight along the coast to try to locate Turkish troops. Afterwards we steamed to Hassani island, where we found the *Suva* and the *Hardinge*.

We were soon told what was in the wind. The Turks were present in some force in the port and town of Wejj, and the idea was that the ships should bombard the place whilst an army of Arabs under the Emir Feisal attacked and drove out the enemy. The *Anne*'s business, of course, was to send up 'planes to 'spot' for the gunners.

On the 20th, therefore, we carried out a practice landing on the island. The ships had detailed a force of about 250 Marines and Bluejackets who were to go ashore to assist the Arabs if necessary. Admiral Wemyss was there in his yacht, the *North Star*, looking on, and the whole affair was rather good fun. After the practice was over I remembered that all the talk was about the sinking of the *Ben-my-chree*, so I sent the Admiral some photos of Castellorizo, for which he thanked me by signal.

Our next duty was to reconnoitre the position of the Turkish trenches, which we did without incident; and there we all lay to await the arrival of Feisal's army. But on the morning of the 23rd there was still no sign of them. So the ships decided to do the job for themselves. Accordingly, all available men were collected – Marines, Bluejackets and stokers – and these, with the help of about 400 Arabs, landed and stormed the town. They did splendidly. They charged the trenches, drove out the Turks, and captured about thirty prisoners. By 2 p.m. they had gained complete possession of the town, and the Turks (or all that was left of them) were beating a hurried retreat northward. Then in the evening up came Feisal, Lawrence, and about 6,000

Arabs. Of course they were too late to do any fighting, but they were in heaps of time to loot – I mean the army, not Feisal and Lawrence – and loot they did, most enthusiastically.

But for us on board the *Anne* the victory was a sad one. We had sent up a 'plane with King as pilot and Stewart of the Royal Scots as observer. They flew for an hour and a half over Wejj and then returned. But when we hoisted them on board we found that poor Stewart was dead. He had been hit by a bullet while leaning forward to send us a wireless message. That evening the chaplain from the *Fox* came on board, and Stewart was buried over the side. All of us felt his loss keenly.

For the next day or two we cruised off the coast, sending up 'planes to try to spot the retreating Turks, but they seemed to have disappeared completely. They must have gone inland and made for the railway. On the 26th January, therefore, we got orders to return to Suez; and so ended my last trip on the *Anne*, where I had had my home for two years.

12

My First Month on the Managem

February–March, 1917

As soon as we arrived in Egypt, after the Wejj victory, I found that all the preliminary arrangements for my new job had been completed, and on the 28th January I was at Port Said going into the matter thoroughly with the Intelligence people. The necessary yacht had been discovered, as I have said before. She was the *Managem*, a small steamer of 160 tons. Her Commander was Morewood of the Egyptian Ports and Lights Administration, and when I first saw her she was manned by an Egyptian crew. I pointed out, however, that we couldn't do the work with Gippies, and so it was arranged that she should be taken over by the Navy, who would man and run her. But I was given to understand that she would be entirely at my own disposal.

On the 4th February I received my official orders to return to military duty – my spy work was to be for the Army and not for the Navy – and to report to Captain Ian Smith, the Intelligence Officer. So, having said goodbye to Samson, I took my four Syrian-Turkish boatmen and went off to my new job.

For the next few days Smith and I were kept at it, preparing schemes for landing and embarking our agents, and interviewing men likely and willing to serve us in that capacity. These were of all kinds and descriptions, and one naturally had to be very careful in making the selections. We knew of people in Syria and Asia Minor who were ready to work for us, either for patriotism or for pay, and the men we wanted were trustworthy and intelligent messengers to get in touch with these; messengers who would be able to understand our instructions, to arrange methods of communication, and to return to us with the kind of information we required. Certainly we did find some good men; but we made one or two mistakes, as will be seen later.

I also spent some time choosing a native boat suitable for surf work, and in getting the hang of some new wireless codes. So it was not until 19th February that I was ready to sail.

On this first trip in the *Managem* Smith came with me. Our object was to land two agents at Athlit, near which place there were some people with whom I had already had dealings, and where I had once landed an agent with whom I had lost touch. We steamed past Athlit, well out to sea, in the afternoon, went on to a point nearly off Haifa, and returned after dark. Then we lowered our boat and I was rowed ashore with the agent – a Jew. This agent I left on land, and returned safely to the ship. There had been no awkward incident of any kind – for which I was devoutly thankful – and we sailed peaceably for Famagusta (Cyprus), where we arrived on the 22nd.

The next day we put to sea again, but the weather became appalling and we had to return. The *Managem* was not the ship for a heavy sea. The cabins were well fitted up, but were below the water-line and badly ventilated. In fact, during the whole of the next two years I was on board, I only slept in my cabin once, and then only when we were in harbour and were able to keep the port-holes open. I used to sleep on a settee in the saloon, or if it was rough and the ship particularly lively, on the floor. The Captain always slept in the charthouse.

On the 27th February the weather was better and we put out to sea. We had with us on board an old native Syrian – he must have been about seventy – whom I intended to land somewhere near the town of Es-Surr (the Tyre of the Bible), giving him messages for certain friends of ours who lived not far from there.

The first night, however, we did not pick up the place until nearly dawn, so we abandoned the attempt for the time being and stood out to sea.

The next night we were luckier, and picked Es-Surr at 2 a.m. I left the ship lying about three miles off the coast, put the old man in my boat, rowed in through a heavy surf, landed him safely, and got back to the ship about four o'clock. Immediately I left the ship on any of these expeditions I used to look back and pick up a star, so that I was certain of some guidance when returning. Another thing I insisted on was a Lewis gun in the stem-sheets of the boat, and I always carried a rifle and revolver. For these night stunts I used to wear a blue jersey, an army tunic and cap, dark flannel trousers and a pair of tennis shoes. When we reached the edge of the surf – if it was not too heavy – I used to turn the boat round, drop an anchor and pay out, letting her drift in to shore stern first; then I would check her a few yards from the beach, keeping her afloat in case we were attacked and had to run for it, and get into the water and swim or wade ashore. Of course, when the surf was heavy we could not use the anchor, and had simply to trust to luck and run the boat through the surf and up the beach. This was always a most nervy business, and we never knew until the last moment that we were not running headlong into the arms of a Turkish patrol – and once in the surf there was no turning back. On a dark, windy night the noise of the surf was terrifying in itself, and often we thumped down on the beach with the boat half-full of water. Once we were actually capsized, but my Turkish boatmen were like fish in the water.

Even at the comparatively early date when we landed our old agent at Surr I was very pleased with these boatmen of mine – a father and three sons. They certainly understood the management of a boat in the surf, and they knew every inch of the coast. Surr was their native town; and their wives and children, who had been without news of them since early in 1915, were still living there. Naturally my boatmen were anxious to let their families know that they were alive and well; and I told our old man, 'el Agooz', or 'the aged one', we called him, to try to get in touch with some of their relatives.

The 'Agooz' was a plucky old fellow. When behind the Turkish lines he used to go about disguised as a beggar; and certainly he looked the part, for his clothes were nothing but a bundle of rags. Before leaving him I told him that we would call at the same place and pick him up, if he were still alive, in about three weeks' time. He went off quite contentedly.

There was nothing further for us to do but to return to Port Said; which we did, arriving on 3rd March, after a very rough voyage. Alhough most of our Bluejackets had worked in trawlers, nearly all of them were sick. In fact, I think I was the only man (with the exception of Captain Cain) in the *Managem* during the war who was never seasick. But if I had not been a good sailor I should never have been able to stick out my job. Apropos of Bluejackets, at one time out of a crew of twenty we had six Irishmen. One of them was rather a character. Going on deck one day, I found him on his knees drawing a map with a piece of chalk and apparently giving a lesson in geography to a Syrian boy of fourteen years of age whom we had captured with his father. Just as I approached I heard the following: 'Dimaithry' (the boy's name was Dimitri), 'there's Ireland,' the Bluejacket pointed out. 'Where England?' from Dimitri. 'Arrah, hould yer whist' – with a smack on the head – 'I'm talking of the ould Counthry, and when you grow up, Dimaithry, yer to jine the Irish Navy!' 'Yessir,' from Dimitri.

For the next two weeks we stayed quietly in harbour. Naturally it was only on moonless nights that we could go ashore to land or embark our agents, so we had to spend a good deal of time in port. Of course, people on shore were always asking what I was doing with the *Managem*, and I used to explain that it was our business to hunt for submarines. This satisfied most of the questioners; but one day when I had been some time on the ship, the Commandant of Police – Colonel Grant – asked me what the moon had to do with submarine-spotting, as he had noticed that I was always at sea when there was no moon or only a new one. That stumped me, and I had to take refuge in a fatuous silence – a silence that I felt quite sure he understood perfectly. But, everything considered, my holidays in port were pleasant enough; and most of my days I spent in golfing or playing tennis, finishing up in the evenings with a game of snooker at the Union Club. In fact, speaking generally, my life was one of ease punctuated by moments of intense fear.

On the 17th March – St Patrick's Day – we sailed. Captain Ian Smith, MC, my OC, was again with me, and we had two agents also on board. I remember one of them wore large, round glasses. We christened him – or rather called him, as he was a Jew – 'The Owl'. The other was a weak-kneed Syrian gentleman, who did not look as if he had much 'guts'. Later we found out he did not belie his appearance.

We intended to put 'The Owl' ashore at Athlit; but when we got there we found that landing was impossible owing to the heavy surf, so we stood out to sea and waited for the next night. But the fates were against us. A heavy sea got up, and we decided to run for Cyprus – which was an invaluable base as it was only ninety miles from the Syrian coast. We arrived at Famagusta on the 19th, and I think everyone was glad when we 'dropped the hook' in the harbour. Our two agents were perfect wrecks.

On the 22nd the *Anne* sent us a wireless to say that the weather was good on the Syrian coast, so we sailed again in the evening. We picked up Athlit about 10.30, and I landed 'The Owl' and saw him on his way to the Jewish colony; after which I returned to the boat and lay off about 200 yards from the beach to await his return. (I had given him a shaded electric torch with which he was to signal when he wanted us to pick him up.) I had been waiting quietly for some time, when to my horror I saw the *Managem* looming nearer and nearer through the dark. She was drifting right down on us. I had asked the Captain to lie about 2½ miles off the shore, and yet there was the ship within a furlong of the beach. I dared not shout, but had to wait until they were nearly on top of us. Then I hailed as quietly as I could and asked the Captain (not very politely) what the devil he was doing. Luckily he heard, and the ship sheered off. If she had bumped the shore we should all have been done for, as the next morning the Turks would have brought up a field-gun and blown us to smithereens. It would have been no good surrendering, as probably we should then have been hanged as spies. Anyhow, my

Turkish boatmen would have been hanged – but not before they had been tortured in some nice way: perhaps by having hot eggs stuck under their armpits, or by being bastinadoed, or by having pieces of skin pulled from their arms and legs – just to induce them to give away the people who were helping us. The Turks used pleasant methods, But all's well that ends well, and, as I have said, the ship sheered off just in time.

'The Owl' returned all right, but said that he would stay at the Jewish colony for the night, so we left him and pulled back to the *Managem*. The next night we brought back 'The Owl' with a good fat report about the enemy's movements – although we had a good deal of trouble in finding the ship, as it was very dark and cloudy and no lights could be shown on board.

I have said that we brought with us from Port Said another 'agent' as well as 'The Owl', and perhaps I had better say here what became of him. In Egypt he had been full of courage and told me that he looked upon himself as a Messiah, as he was going to take the news to his friends on shore that they would soon be delivered from the Turkish yoke. But, once at sea, this courage of his soon evaporated. When I went to give him his instructions I found him in a pitiful state of sheer funk. He was lying in his bunk with an open Bible upside down – on his chest, praying between intervals of seasickness. When the time came for him to go on shore with me in the boat he was in such a state of terror that I had to abandon all idea of landing him. Eventually I got rid of him at Cyprus, whence he was shipped back to Egypt.

To return to my story. When I picked up 'The Owl' we made for Es-Surr, and I landed at the place where I had instructed 'The Agooz' to meet me. But there was no sign of him, nor was there any message in a 'post-box' I had buried there. So I had to return to the ship, hoping that he had not been captured. On 28th March, however, I determined to have another shot at picking him up. I liked the plucky old fellow, and I did not want him to think that we had abandoned him. Back, therefore, we sailed. I landed at 2 p.m. on the 30th and made an exhaustive search of the beach and of the brushwood near it, but all to no purpose. After this I could do no more; and, having returned to the ship, I gave the order to make for Port Said. There was too much moon for us to stay 'submarine hunting' any longer.

13

Spies and Agents

April–June, 1917

ONE OF THE FIRST THINGS I had to think about when we were once more peacefully in harbour was the means of supplying our agents with revolvers and ammunition. Thinking that I might find what I wanted at the Customs, I went to Alexandria and tackled the Director-General. He certainly gave me permission to take anything I liked from his store, and one of his people showed me revolvers of every kind and description, which had been confiscated from travellers landing in the country. But there was no ammunition for them, and so, as I had to go to Cairo to talk shop with the GHQ Intellince people I determined to try again there. At Cairo, as a matter of fact, I did get what I wanted, for I was able to purchase both revolvers and ammunition from the Egyptian police stores. But I had to file off all Government marks from the revolvers in case any of my men were caught armed with them.

I got back to Port Said on the 14th April, and sailed the same evening for Athlit, taking two agents with me. We ran up the coast north of Haifa, came back at dark, made Mount Carmel and then ran down to Athlit. The ship lay off about three miles, and I went ashore with the 'agent', landed him safely and waited. After a while he returned to the shore, bringing with him his sister 'Sarah'; and we got safely back to the ship, having been away four hours. Luckily we had a calm sea and a dark night.

We next pushed off for Famagusta. In spite of the fine weather all our 'agents' were seasick, including 'Sarah'. We arrived at Famagusta next day, and from 5 a.m. till midnight I was busy coding and sending away all the information we had obtained. How I hated coding!

For the following two days I was busy interviewing likely agents to use on the Asia Minor and Syrian coast. These people had to come to the house we had rented outside Famagusta under cover of darkness, as there was no doubt that amongst such a population as that of Cyprus the enemy had a good many friends and probably paid spies.

We had intended to sail the next day, but the sea got up and a regular storm blew, so that it was no good even thinking of making a landing. At last we sailed, on the 26th April, and ran over to Athlit, but there still was too much of a sea running for me to land, while the glass was falling rapidly. I felt pretty certain that we should not do much by waiting about, and so decided to make for Port Said.

On the 14th May, Morewood, our Captain, gave up the command, as he was wanted back by the Ports and Lights. To replace him on board the *Managem* we were given Lieut. Cain, RNR, who had previously been assisting the RNO at Navy House. Cain was a first-class man. Originally he hailed from the Isle of Man. He had been 'in sail'; and afterwards, just before the war, had been skipper of a New Zealand Union Steamship Co. steamer. He had an extra-Master's certificate and was a real stout-hearted fellow.

I should have mentioned before this that as well as the British captain we carried a pilot for the Syrian coast. The latter was Captain Angoras – a Greek – who formerly had been a captain of one of the Khedival Line steamers plying on the Syrian coast. He was an excellent fellow and knew the coast well; but after a couple of trips Cain came to the conclusion that he did not want any help, and so Captain Angoras was no longer retained.

On the 16th May we shipped a couple of agents and put to sea. The 'agents' consisted of two males and one female, and a basket of carrier pigeons. The humans I hoped to land at Athlit; and the pigeons I let loose next day when off Abu Zebura, as an experiment. We were having shocking weather, and any idea of landing the agents had to be abandoned; and, as the weather got worse, we had to run for safety to Famagusta. We were very fortunate to get there, too. No sooner had we got into the harbour than a regular cyclone came on, the worst storm known for years in these parts. I happened to be on shore in the evening, and on coming down to the quay found it was too bad to put off to the ship; so, having collected all our ' liberty' men, I took them on board the French tender *Laborieux* that was lying alongside the quay and spent the night on board her.

Next day we were able to join our ship and, having got my agents on board, we sailed for Es-Surr. That night I rowed right into the little harbour and went on shore. The houses ran right down to the water's edge, and the one I wanted to reach was only about a hundred yards from the shore. We beached the boat safely without being seen and, taking one of my boatmen with me, I landed to spy out the position. I was just crawling round the corner of a house when I heard a shout of 'Min Gai – who goes there?' Needless to say, I lay low, and after a minute or so poked my head round the corner of the building, holding my rifle ready. I could just make out the figure of a man, also with a rifle in his hand, who, when he saw me, whisked back round his corner. The position might have been amusing if it had not been so unhealthily exciting. But as things stood I did not enjoy myself at all. Knowing that it would only give away our friends in the town if I stayed, I crept back to my boatman and whispered to him that we must make for the boat. When, however, we reached the shore, we found that our boatmen and our boat were no longer there. The former had pushed off when they heard the challenge. So there was nothing for it but to swim – taking care not to splash. Every minute I expected a volley to be fired at us from the shore. But luckily our boatmen waited for us about fifty yards out, and we got on board safe and sound. So far, so good. But now to complicate matters a heavy squall came on, the sea got up, and the waves broke into the boat, half filling her with water. So there we were with a water-logged boat on a lee shore with the Turks waiting for us on the beach. Luckily it was a very dark night; and, knowing that it was hopeless to try and reach the ship, we pulled as hard as we could to a reef which showed just above water, about five hundred yards from the shore. I had just made up my mind to scramble on to this reef and hang on there until daylight, in the hope that the ship would then spot us and get us out of our fix before the Turks could capture us, when the wind suddenly dropped and the sea calmed down. We reached the ship when all on board had given us up for lost; and very glad we were to reach her at all.

We could do no more at Suïr for the time being, so we sailed for Famagusta and arrived there on the 23rd May.

At this time of the war, while I was carrying out an espionage on the Syrian coast, Lieut. Salter, who was attached to our Intelligence office in Cyprus, was carrying out similar work on the Asia Minor coast. As we only had the one ship, he used to do his landing from French trawlers. All the French battleships and large cruisers comprising the blockading squadron of the Syrian coast had, since the submarining of the *Amiral Charner*, been replaced by destroyers and trawlers. These latter were commanded by junior French naval lieutenants, and very decent fellows they were – most willing and obliging. While we were lying in Famagusta, one of these French trawlers came in with Lieut. Salter, who had just landed an agent successfully at Mersina. This agent was to get in touch with a 'friendly' (at a price) person at Adana, who, once a month, would send a report down to the coast, to an agreed spot, where we could land and collect it. It was extremely important to have an agent watching the railway before it reached Aleppo, as we were thus able to calculate, by referring to our reports of movement on the SyrianPalestine line, how many troops had been sent down towards Ras el Ain to reinforce the enemy in Mesopotamia.

The French boat *Laborieux*, with Captain Picard on board, now came in. This officer was in charge of the French Intelligence. He was a good fellow, and we were great friends.

On the 28th May, while we were still weatherbound in Cyprus, a German aeroplane flew over the harbour at a height of about five thousand feet and proceeded towards Larnaca. It had come, presumably, to observe if any military camps, etc., were being formed in the island. This was the first appearance of an enemy's aeroplane over the island, and it was up to us to find out whence it came. This we did later, receiving from our agents the information that an aerodrome had been erected at Selefke, on the Asia Minor coast, just north of Cyprus.

On the 29th we sailed for Port Said, hugging the Syrian coast and picking up signals at Athlit, which informed us that 'all was well' with our friends ashore there. On the morning of the 31st, when about twenty-five miles off Port Said, we sighted a large steamer which appeared to be slowly sinking. We closed with her and found she was the BI boat *Ozarda*, which had just been submarined. Her crew were in the boats alongside, and as she had two or three small steamers from Port Said to assist her, we steamed on into harbour. Eventually the *Ozarda* was towed in and grounded.

As we were going to be in Port Said for a few days, I took the train to Alexandria and visited various departments at the harbour in search of a suitable boat for surf work. But there was nothing doing, so I returned to Port Said and sailed in the *Managem* on 13th June.

This trip I took with me some carrier pigeons to try, and when off Abu Zebora, we let them go. They all reached Port Said safely. On the night of the 15th we ran in towards Athlit. I went away in one boat with the agents, and another filled with stores (which consisted of bombs, rifles and ammunition) followed. I instructed the boat with stores to anchor about three hundred yards off the beach, and then went ashore with 'Sarah' and Yussef (our agents). They walked up to the house to bring down help to unload and conceal the stores, while I remained on shore. After about an hour and a half they returned, and I then pulled off to the stores boat, brought all the stuff on shore, and handed it over to them. Luckily there was not much surf. Having received all the reports for the last three weeks I returned to the ship. In connection with this landing I might mention that it was the only time I ever took a British Bluejacket with me, and even then I only left him in the stores boat and never asked him to land. Yet, when we came to censor the man's letters, we found that he had written a marvellous account of the night. According to him, both he and I had landed under heavy rifle fire, concealed ourselves behind rocks, returned enemy's fire, driven off enemy, and then swam out to the boats, having to sink our rifles on the way, and had been hauled on board in an exhausted condition. We had – according to him – slain several Turks. He appeared to be very bloodthirsty; but this was accounted for, perhaps, by the fact that before the war he had been a ship's butcher!

From Athlit we ran to Famagusta, where I spent a day coding and cabling to GHQ the reports I had brought off – or, at any rate, the most interesting items of them concerning movements of troops, etc. Next day (18th June), having shipped another 'agent' ('agent' sounded nicer than 'spy'), we sailed for Es-Surr (Tyre). The sea began to get up, and the Captain thought it would be impossible for me to make a night landing, and that we ought to return to Famagusta. But we consulted Sasseen – my best boatman – and he advised going on, as we would be sheltered by the reef when landing. So go on we did; and although there was still a heavy sea running when we got there at 10.30 p.m., we lowered our boat, and I pushed off for the town with the four Syrians pulling. We took a ladder with us and, on getting into the little harbour, put it in the water – leaving the boat lying about 150 yards off the shore – and three of us swam to the land. Then we crawled with our ladder to a house in which lived one of Sasseen's friends. Here we put up our ladder, which Sasseen climbed and tapped at the window until it was opened. He was recognised at once, and we found no difficulty in getting into touch with the people of the house. They were quite willing to get us the information we wanted, and I told them when to look out for us again. One of the girls of the house very pluckily went out into the town and brought back one of Sasseen's sisters, who naturally was delighted to see him. We found out from her that the old 'Agooz' was still alive and well, and I gave her instructions for him which included arrangements to get him away. Then, having finished everything to my satisfaction, we took down the ladder, swam back to our boat, and eventually reached the *Managem* without having been seen by the enemy. We had been right inside a town held by the Turks and had stayed there for some time. However pleasant such a stunt may be to read about in a book of adventure, it is not the kind of thing actually to do for a holiday amusement.

We now sailed for Port Said and called at Athlit *en route* to pick up reports. I went in as usual in the boat with an agent, but when we reached the edge of the surf we found that the broken water was too rough for the boat to get through it; so one of my boatmen volunteered to swim ashore and take the agent with him. This he did, and both men reached the beach in safety, returning after about a couple of hours. Just as the agent was alongside he suddenly started to shriek at the top of his voice that he was drowning. There was nothing for it but to reach out and hold his head under water, so that he could not be heard on land. When he had quieted down a bit I hauled him on board – but not before. It took him some time to recover, and we were back on the *Managem* before he could tell me that the report had not yet arrived, and that our friends had asked that we should return a couple of nights later.

To fill in the time we ran to Famagusta and returned to Athlit on the 26th June. I landed with two men and walked to the rendezvous, but no one was there. We waited for some time and then decided to return to the boat. But on the way back we were given a good scare. Suddenly shots were fired at us, and the bullets whistled uncomfortably close to our heads. It was one of the many moments when I felt a cold distaste for all warfare – and especially for agent-running. But our attackers did not show themselves, and we got safely away. Yet I felt very friendly towards Port Said harbour when we arrived there a day later. I had had enough excitement to last me for some little time.

There is one thing of interest I think I should mention in connection with cruising in the *Managem*. Once, when returning to Port Said and when half-way between Cyprus and that port, we sighted a curious-looking object one afternoon at a great height up in the sky. It was not an aeroplane. Suddenly it dawned on us what it was; nothing more or less than a Zeppelin! We reported what we had seen on our arrival and heard no more about it. I don't think our report was believed at the time. As a matter of fact, this was the Zeppelin that made the famous flight from Bucharest to German East Africa and back via the Libyan Desert, Khartoum and Sudan. In my opinion, one of the most wonderful achievements of the war.

14

Agents Adventurous

July–September, 1917

WHILE I WAS in Port Said I used to turn up at the Intelligence Office every day and try to scrape together all the bits of information which might be useful to us on our voyages. News of minefields and of submarines was of course especially important. I had no wish to blunder against either one or the other if I could possibly help it. My experience when the *Anne* was torpedoed had not been so pleasant that I wished it repeated, and the *Managem* would not have stood the ghost of a chance if she had been hit by anything heavier than a baby's rattle.

On the 13th July we were off again. I had some carrier pigeons with me which I intended to pass on to our agents at Athlit for use with urgent messages. But our old enemy, a heavy sea, forced me to postpone my visit – but not before I had been nearly swamped on the edge of the surf. So we made for Famagusta, passing a Jewish colony near enough to spot an 'all's well' window signal from our friends there.

At Famagusta I left my agents and the pigeons, and sailed for Tyre on July 17th, going ashore the same night.

This time we rowed right into the little harbour, and landed bang alongside the house I wanted. I met our friend and suggested to him that we should lay a telephone (submarine) line from his house – against which the sea washed – run it past the reefs a mile or so out, and attach the seaward end to a small float. The idea (Captain Smith's) was that, instead of having to land in order to get news, we could run in at night, pick up the telephone line at the float, and talk to him. He thought it a great idea, but on questioning him I found that fishermen sometimes waded along in the sea past his house, with cast nets. This, of course, made the whole scheme impossible; for if one of the fishermen tripped over the line he would naturally trace it to the house, and then it would have been all up with our friends.

After returning to Famagusta to pick up our agent, I next made another effort to get on shore at Athlit. This time I was successful and came away with a fat report, which took me a whole day to translate (nearly all the information was written in French) and code. But I did not get rid of my pigeons until a couple of days later, when I again landed. That night on the beach I realised how loudly pigeons can coo. It seemed to me that the little brutes made enough noise to bring half the Turkish army down on me. But the Turks must have been very sound asleep, and I handed the birds safely over to our friends on shore – finding that we had been very lucky not to arrive a day earlier. For the man I met told me that a German submarine had arrived at Athlit the day previous, and that some of her crew had landed for provisions. I was glad we had missed her.

On the 26th July we were once more safely at Famagusta. While we had been at sea, Salter and another man (Smithers) had run across to Provincial Island, a small rocky islet about a mile from the Asia Minor coast, on a French trawler. They had landed there and had spent a few days watching the coast with their glasses for any signs of Turkish troops or German submarines. They had arranged to be picked up by a French ship, but she never turned up. Eventually, as provisions were running short, Salter launched the small dinghy they had with them and sailed for Cyprus, seventy miles away. He got there safely, and very lucky he was to do so.

While we were lying in harbour one of our stokers, who was on a 'spree' ashore, fell off the town ramparts – a drop of at least 40 feet – and injured his spine. We had to leave him behind in hospital. The poor fellow never recovered the use of his limbs, and died in England some months later. The curious thing was that his name was MacLoughlin, and that only a short time before I had been told about another MacLoughlin who had fallen off the ramparts at Nicosia, but had picked himself up and walked home none the worse for his fall! In justice to Mac No. 2, I should mention that he had *not* been on the 'spree'.

We sailed on the 29th July for Provincial Island, in order to take off the second man who had been left there. Major Smith came with us. Arriving there at about 9 p.m., we lowered a boat, rowed in and took off our man. We had previously received news of a Turkish official who was anxious to desert, and we had made arrangements, through our agents, for him to be at a certain spot on the night of the 30th. Having reached the appointed place in the dark, we sent away a boat manned by three Asia Minor Greeks who were employed by us. They did not return, and eventually we picked them up miles out at sea – and very pleased they were at our finding them, as they had no water or provisions in the boat. Apparently they had landed all right, but our Turkish friend had never turned up. They had waited a couple of hours, and had then tried to find the ship, but missed her in the dark.

On the 3rd August we were back in Port Said, where, as it was nearly full moon, we had to wait for the next ten days. On the 13th, however, we headed for Athlit – I was beginning to know the place pretty well by now – with agents and a large supply of gold. (Speaking about the latter, I may mention that we always paid our way with sovereigns, and we had to be very careful that none of these were dated later than 1914. The possession of English money of a later year might have been awkward for our friends on shore, and would certainly have aroused the suspicions of the enemy.) This time I did my job successfully, picked up reports and made for Famagusta to code them.

I now determined to have another try at getting the 'Agooz' away from Tyre, and so sailed on the 16th August for that place. We arrived about midnight, and I went off in my boat. Off the entrance to the small harbour we lay to, while two of my Syrians swam to the shore. Shortly after they had left us we saw, to our horror, a large schooner within a few yards of us. I hurriedly trained the Lewis gun on her, but of course the last thing I wanted to do was to fire, as that would have aroused the town and given away the whole show. Moreover, our two men ashore would then certainly have been captured. But we were in luck. The schooner was running for the harbour, and her sails were between us and her crew – who never saw us! So we followed her closely, and saw her drop her anchor and her crew go ashore.

Then for a little while we lay quiet, waiting. But it was not long before I saw our two men swimming towards us. As soon as they were on board they told me that they had got to the house where the 'Agooz' was, and had brought him down to the harbour, where he was lying concealed behind some rocks. We waited again until we were sure that all was quiet, and then paddled silently into the harbour, ran ashore, landed, found the old man, brought him to the boat, and got away in safety to the ship. We had had quite an exciting night.

The poor old 'Agooz' was full of pluck, but only a shadow of his former self, which was only natural as he had been for nearly six months in a famine-stricken country. He had carried out successfully all the instructions I had given him.

Famagusta was for us something in the nature of a harbour of refuge, and thither we returned. But there was no peace for us, and, shipping two agents, we sailed again on the 22nd. It was another Athlit job, and, like many others of the same kind, could not be carried out owing to heavy weather. With anything like a sea running the surf there formed an impassable barrier and, as often as not, we could not reach the shore.

Before we left Cyprus, Abdulla, my head Syrian boatman, had come to me in a great state. Apparently a short time before we arrived a schooner belonging to some Cypriot Turks had escaped from Famagusta and had gone over to the enemy. My man knew one of the crew, and said that this man was sure to inform the Turkish authorities that he, the boatman, was working with me in the *Managem*. He pointed out that as soon as the Turks knew this they would take vengeance on his womenfolk who were still in Es-

Surr, and would probably hang them and burn their houses. He implored me to try to rescue them.

At first I hesitated, as it meant that if we were successful and brought the women away we should never again be able to use Es-Surr as a landing-place, for the Turks would then certainly be on the look out for us there. After considering the whole matter carefully, however, I came to the conclusion that if I did not make the attempt and the women were hanged my boatmen would never work for me again – and they had been absolutely faithful ever since we captured them. So I told Abdulla that I would have a shot at it and do my best.

Actually things went well. We reached Surr about 11 p.m., and went off as usual in the boat. We landed without incident, crawled up to the town in single file, and scratched at a window in Abdulla's house. Immediately it was opened we told the inmates that they must come at once, just as they were, and leave all their belongings behind. They came all right, and we started off creeping down the street towards the sea, calling at another house on the way to repeat the process. But here we were not quite so lucky. One old lady – the grandmother – absolutely refused to budge, and threatened that if we tried to carry her with us by force she would scream. We had not the time to argue, and we couldn't risk her screams, so she carried her point and stayed where she was. But there were quite enough of us without her. The whole crowd numbered sixteen, including a baby and about three children, all in their nightdresses. They were extraordinarily plucky, in fact the girl I was with seemed to find the whole affair amusing and started to giggle. I was glad she was enjoying herself, I most certainly was not. But I could not help thinking of the Rape of the Sabines.

As we crawled past the house of the Kaimakam – the Governor – I spotted that gentleman sitting on his verandah smoking a cigarette, and Sasseen suggested in a whisper that we should capture him and take him with us. I fell in with the suggestion at first and told Sasseen to cough, open the gate and call out that he wanted to speak to the Governor. Then when the latter came down the path

I would jam a revolver against his head and bring him along. On second thoughts, however, I decided that this plan was too risky as the women were only half-way to the shore; so, much against our will, we left the Turk to finish his cigarette in peace and liberty.

For the rest, there was not a hitch in our plans. We got the whole crowd on board the boat – we had brought a big one – and pushed off for the ship, which we reached safely. It had been a good night's work.

The surf was still too heavy for us to make a landing on the unprotected Athlit beach, and as we were a very crowded ship, and as anyway our passengers were not clothed for a prolonged voyage, we made straight for Port Said, where we arrived on August 26th and bade farewell to our guests. They were all extremely grateful and, on leaving the ship, kissed our hands, and even tried to kiss our boots.

For the next month we had bad luck with the weather. Twice I tried to land, once at Athlit and once at Ras el Nakura, where I wanted to establish a branch, so to speak; but on both occasions the surf beat me and we had to run for Cyprus. The first time we had the consolation of capturing a schooner. She did not exactly belong to the enemy – she was a Cypriot – but when we sighted her she was heading north-east for enemy territory, and the Captain did not explain the reason satisfactorily. So we took her in tow and saw her safely into Famagusta. A few Cypriot schooners had already gone over to the Turks and supplied them with information, and we were not going to watch another added to the list right under our eyes.

On the 21st September, the weather improved, and that night I managed at last to land an agent at Athlit. The next night we picked him up again and I listened to his news, which was not altogether good. It appeared that the Jewish colony were becoming nervous and that they wished us to take them out of the country. This gave me food for thought, and I decided to make for Famagusta and report to GHQ, and also to seek aid from the *Veresis*, a trawler which had been lately attached to the Intelligence and was used for the same kind of work as ourselves, but for the most part further to the north. With her help I knew that, if all went well, we could 'evacuate' the whole Jewish colony.

Luckily the *Veresis* was in port, and, having received orders from GHQ, we sailed again in her company on the 25th. At 1 a.m. that same night I landed to look into the situation on shore, but I was informed that the colony now felt safer and would stay where they were. The wife of one of our agents, however, had elected to leave, and brought her child with her to the boat. I took them on board. The poor little kiddie never uttered a sound until we were well clear of the shore, when he turned, said something to his mother and began to sob. I asked what he wanted – he was a little chap of about five years old – and the mother explained that when they had been creeping from her house to the shore she had warned him that he was not to cry or make a sound. He had been most obedient, and had never uttered a murmur until that minute, when he asked, 'Mummy, may I cry now?' She had given him permission, and the sobs were the result.

Amongst my many night trips to the shore I had on one occasion to meet a deserting Turkish officer. When I rendezvoused with him behind a rock in the dark he thrust something into my hand. I took him off to the ship and then examined the article he had given me. It was his Masonic lodge certificate!

Another time when ashore one of our 'agents' informed me that there was a certain British officer a prisoner not very far distant, and he thought he could effect his escape if I could let him have three hundred guineas with which to cover what we might call 'travelling expenses', which meant bribes for the guards, and of these guineas no doubt a fair, or probably unfair, proportion would stick to his palm. I told him I would let him know what to do in the matter during the next few days. I returned to the ship and sent a wireless to 'The Authorities', asking if I should attempt to carry out the rescue. I received a reply, short and to the point, 'Not necessary!' Wild horses would not drag from me the name of that poor officer; at any rate he is quite safe now and alive and kicking.

We were on the whole extraordinarily lucky with our 'agents'. I don't think more than seven were actually captured. Six of these were hanged and one had his head cut off. I received a letter after the war from the British naval authorities asking me for remarks on a letter they enclosed. This was from a man who said his brother had been landed by 'Captain Weldon, of the British dreadnought *Managem* [he should apologise to all dreadnoughts; the poor little *Managem*'s tonnage amounted to only 160 tons!], on the Syrian coast. He had been captured by the Turks and hanged. He had left on board the *Managem*, with Captain Weldon, a portmanteau containing clothing and £500 in gold. Would the Admiral kindly order Captain Weldon to return them to writer?' Anyway, that was the gist of it. My reply was that certainly the man in question had been landed, and had been captured and hanged. He had volunteered. I had made all arrangements, and he was landed from a French trawler, not the dreadnought *Managem*. I had informed him I would be in the *Managem* at a certain spot on the coast three nights after his being landed to take him off again, and instructed him to make certain signals. The night after he was landed by the Frenchmen I went ashore not far off, and was informed a certain man had been captured who had been put ashore from a ship, had been tortured by the Turks, and had told them he was to be called for on such and such a night, and also told them all about the signals! My informant asked me if I knew anything about it, as if a boat came in for the man the Turks were going to have fifty soldiers on the beach waiting to fire on it when it grounded. I expressed absolute ignorance of the matter and returned to the *Managem*. On the appointed night I pulled in in my boat to within 500 yards of the rendezvous (it was a dark night). Sure enough the agreed-on signals were made, but not quite correctly. It was a cold night, and I suppose the Turks got impatient, and the way they went on with rapid and anxious efforts to induce me to go ashore brought to my mind that old nursery rhyme, 'Dilly, dilly, dilly, come and be killed'. I didn't. I returned to the *Managem*. I never saw the £500 in gold. As a matter of fact, if it had ever been with the man on board the trawler he must have taken it to his friends ashore, and Johnnie Turk got it.

15

The Daily Round

October, 1917–January, 1918

EARLY IN OCTOBER, when we were lying in Port Said, I was sent for by Rear Admiral Jackson, the new Admiral of the station. He was most pleasant, and seemed to take a genuine interest in our work. This heartened us considerably.

A few days later I went up to Cairo and saw Edmunds, who was in charge of the EMSIB, the Eastern Mediterranean Special Intelligence Bureau. He also was very kind, and even flattering. He was an exceedingly capable man, and had put in a lot of real hard work, for which he was never properly thanked. He was one of the few people with whom I had dealings who seemed really to understand what my job was.

We had not got rid of the idea that the colony at Athlit might have to be 'evacuated', and on the 12th October we sailed, in company with the *Veresis*, to look further into the matter. That night we landed an agent, but he was not met, and returned to the ship. The night after we wanted to try again, but were baulked by a fog which prevented us from finding our landing-place; so the third night we determined to settle the matter and sent three agents ashore. They went right up to the colony, but returned after about two hours and reported that as far as they could see the place was deserted. This made us uneasy, and the following day we steamed close in to the coast, as if we were out on a casual cruise, and had a good look at the village through our glasses. But neither near the houses nor in the fields could we see a sign of life, and we had to admit that in all probability the Turks had become suspicious and undertaken a raid. Later we heard that this surmise was at least partially correct. The Turks had raided and had seized 'Sarah', one of our two chief agents. Yussef, the other, managed to escape. The Turks were very anxious to learn what 'Sarah' had been doing, the method by which she communicated with us, and the names of her accomplices, and the Turkish methods of interrogating were not pleasant. They did not shrink from torture. But 'Sarah' was game to the end. She refused to tell her tormentors anything, and at last, seizing the rifle of one of her guards, she shot herself. Such a suicide finds honour in the Valhalla of brave women.

Yussef's end was no less splendid. He had evaded the Turks when they swooped down on the village. There was nothing to stop him from making his way to the shore, where he would have stood a good chance of being picked up by us in the *Managem*. But – well, the Turks issued a proclamation that they would massacre the whole Jewish colony unless he gave himself up: and Yussef was hanged. He surrendered voluntarily, and went to his own death rather than let his friends suffer. Englishmen often talk about 'playing the game', but even during the war few Britishers played it to a finer finish than this Jewish girl and Yussef.

I have spoken of Turkish tortures and their way with captured spies. Let me digress and give an example, of which the result was grimly humorous. One of our 'agents' was captured near Mersina. He was taken to Adana and there tortured, with the object of making him give the names of all the people he knew who were helping the British. This agent was not of the stuff of which martyrs are made, and after a few pieces of skin had been pulled from his arms and legs he said he would tell his captors all they required. But if he was not a stoic, he was not a fool. He gave the Turks eighty names, but not one of these names belonged to a person who had anything to do with the Allies. *He* is still alive, but I shouldn't be surprised if eighty of his personal enemies are dead. To return to my story. When I got back from our last Athlit trip I retired to hospital. The doctor said that there was nothing wrong, but that I wanted a rest. I got it. I slept for three days and three nights, only waking for an occasional meal, and at the end of that time I felt like the proverbial giant refreshed. I needed the feeling, for Major Ian Smith was ordered to GHQ, and I had to take over his job in addition to my own.

An amusing incident occurred in connection with my shore office. One day the telephone rang, and a voice said, 'Is that Captain Weldon?' I replied, 'Yes.' The voice said, 'Tell me, are you a naval or a military officer?' I, thinking it was someone pulling my leg, replied, 'Oh, call me a French Marine!' I then heard a rather angry voice saying, 'What do you mean, sir?' and realised it was some big bug from GHQ speaking. I hurriedly said 'Military,' and rang off. We sailed again on the 11th November, having taken on board three agents. These men were natives of Morocco, and we had put them through a course of incendiarism, such as the setting of time bombs, and had armed them with harmless-looking eggs and cigarettes which, when broken or half burnt through, would burst into flames and set fire to any inflammable matter with which they might come into contact. The idea was that I was to land them on the coast well behind the Turkish lines, when they were to wander round making as much havoc as they could among such things as large dumps of ammunition, forage and aerodromes.

On our way up the coast we called in at Deir el Belah. When we got within five miles of this place we noticed that the whole surface of the sea was covered with oil, and shortly afterwards we picked up a ship's raft and two wardroom chairs. (Incidentally, I am at the moment sitting on one of them, in the middle of Ireland!) On the raft was lying a cane chair, which I recognised as belonging to Leslie, the Lieut.-Commander of 'Monitor 15'. We closed with some transports lying off the coast, and heard that a few hours previously an enemy submarine had torpedoed this monitor, and also the torpedo-boat destroyer *Staunch*. Several lives were lost. I heard a year later that the German submarine which had done this had been captured, and that Leslie, who was on leave, was shown her log at the Admiralty. The log described how she had waited for hours outside the net defences at Deir el Belah and watched through her periscope transports and trawlers going in and out. Having thus made sure of the passage between the nets, she came in herself, sank the monitor and the torpedo-boat destroyer, and got out again. It was a fine piece of work for the Hun.

We passed Saida ('Sidon' of the Bible) on the 14th, and that night I went ashore with my three agents and landed them successfully. We had paid them in full, and given them their instructions, which were simple, namely, to do as much damage as they could. They had friends in the country, and said they would stay there, and that there was no need for me to call for them again. That was the last I saw of them. But, curiously enough, shortly after their arrival we heard of dumps of forage having been burnt and of a big fire in an aerodrome that destroyed large quantities of petrol and about twelve aeroplanes. So we assumed that our friends had been busy. At the end of the month, when we had just got back to Port Said – we had been held up in Cyprus owing to a rumoured Austrian naval attack – I heard that Borton Pasha had been appointed Military Governor of Jerusalem and had applied for me to assist him. But GHQ put their foot (or should I say feet?) down. Apparently they had no one to take over my sea work.

At the beginning of December (the 9th) we again put out to sea and, at the end of about eight hours' steaming, ran into a most awful storm. We had a really bad time. During the night I honestly thought we should founder, and I was nearly positive that we looped the loop at least twice. We had bad weather all the next day, and got no sleep until we arrived under the lee of Cyprus. On the morning of the 11th we at last crawled into harbour at Famagusta, and very glad we were, too.

Here we found the *Veresis*. It had been arranged that in future we were to sail in company, as about this time submarines were very busy in these waters. Salter went on board the *Veresis*, and on the 13th we sailed together for Latakia, where we intended to land an agent. When we arrived off the coast there was such a sea running that it was utterly impossible to land, so out we went again and steamed towards Karatash on the Asia Minor coast.

The next morning we steamed along the coast looking out for a suitable landing-place for future work.

The same evening we ran down again to Latakia and Salter went away, successfully landed an agent, waited for him, and brought him back with reports. These reports were very valuable as they came from our agent at Aleppo, and dealt with the movement of troops, not only towards the Syrian front but also towards Mesopotamia. Turkish and German newspapers had also been sent to us.

We now returned to Famagusta, where we were busy for a couple of days writing reports and coding telegrams. On the 20th we tried to do a landing at Tyre, but the sea was too big, and we returned without accomplishing anything. On Christmas Day we were still in Cyprus, and some of our friends on shore invited Cain, the first officer, our 'Snotty' and myself to dinner. On Boxing Day we pushed off back for Port Said.

My chief thought on the first morning of the new year was, I expect, the same as that of many other men, i.e. when was this bloody war going to end? I had last seen my wife and family in Ireland in September, 1914. When I mooted the idea of leave the answer was always, 'Certainly, if you can get a man to carry on for you.' I don't for one minute wish to insinuate that my job was anything wonderful, or even important; apparently it was not, as I started and finished in it as a 'three-star man' (captain), but at the same time one couldn't help feeling in the back of one's mind that it was up to 'them' to find the substitute. Naturally, I did my best, but it was a difficult matter. There were any amount of men who would have volunteered, *but* – anyway at this date – one required a man who was a good sailor, knew a certain amount of Arabic and French (personally, I was bad at both languages), would not rub the Navy – which practically meant, would be tactful in dealing with the ship's captain, because when all was said and done, one had to realise that he was captain of the ship and responsible to the Admiralty for her safety and the safety of the crew – and could be a bit of a diplomat when dealing with the French. As a matter of fact, all that was really required was someone with common sense and tact who wouldn't be seasick at the critical moment. I thought of two men, and tried to get them. One was Captain J.R. Herbert, who had been with me on the *Anne* as an observer, and the other was Glyn Terrell, whom I had formerly known in Cairo. I sent up their names, but apparently Herbert was busy with a new force, the Frontiers District Administration in Sinai, of which district he had had previous experience, trying to get some order into the state of affairs there, whilst Terrell could not be spared by the PWM, Egypt. Either of these men would have jumped at the job. Terrell was a keen yachtsman, and had already done some excellent work towing lighters up to Mudros. But – 'maleesh': no leave. One other man to whom I had written privately, thinking he would do, wrote back and said he fancied the job would suit him very well; but could I tell him if there was much danger attached to it? I didn't answer him.

I think that I have already mentioned that I had been appointed Military Intelligence Officer, Port Said, in the place of Major Smith. This meant that I had a good deal of office work to do, sitting at the end of a telephone. Yet I was expected to go to sea at the same time. In fact I was like the bird (in my case, I presume, a seagull) which should have been able to be in two places at once. I simply had to do the best I could; leave a clerk in charge and notify GSI, GHQ, of my movements.

On January 12th we happened to be in harbour at Cyprus, when the look-out reported a submarine close inshore, and on the surface. Immediately we weighed anchor and started gallantly away to tackle her – and to destroy her, of course. We began to chase her right enough, and then – she dived. That was the last we saw of her. By this time, however, we were armed with depth- charges; so we dropped one. The result was not quite what we had hoped for. The charge certainly exploded, and we, as I thought, went off the water like a seaplane rising. Everything on board that could be upset was upset. Personnel, crockery, glasses, and a hundred and one other odds and ends came crashing down. Apparently depth charges were meant to be dropped by TSDs doing about 27 knots, which could get clear of the explosions. We at the time were doing about

8 knots, and so naturally suffered almost as much as the submarine would have done if she had been there – and she was not.

But we recovered ourselves and kept chasing gallantly round and round after our invisible foe, until Captain Cain remarked that he was damned if he knew whether we were chasing the submarine or the submarine was chasing us. I could not enlighten him, and as we came to the conclusion that we should only damage ourselves if we dropped another depth-charge, we returned to the harbour and adjourned to the club.

On the morning of the 13th, having taken on board an agent, we sailed for Latakia. The same night I took our man in and landed him. I waited by the boat on shore, while he proceeded to the house of one of our friends and returned safely, with all the reports of Latakia district and those from Aleppo. He informed me that the whole crop of Latakia tobacco, which of course could not be exported during the war, was lying there in the town, and that if we could pay about £1,200 we could buy the lot – it was, I believe, worth something like £25,000. We (Salter and I) very naturally suggested that there might be some difficulty in getting it away; but he said, none at all, if we came along at night with a few schooners and squared the authorities (Turks). Of course, we should have been delighted to do so, but, unfortunately, we were not in commerce.

16

Carrying On

February–July, 1918

B Y THIS TIME we had got our espionage work well systematised, and it was now more or less a mere matter of calling regularly at fixed stations and picking up reports. But although calling regularly was all right in the summer months, it was quite the reverse during the winter. The Syrian coast is most exposed, and we finished more than half our trips without having been able to make a landing. We just did our best, however, Salter and the *Veresis* taking for the most part the Asia Minor work, and we ourselves of the *Managem* the Syrian. Although it never lost its uncomfortable excitement, my job had become almost stereotyped; and I only propose here to write of the incidents which were a little out of the common.

As I was now Intelligence Officer, Port Said, I had sometimes to let the *Managem* sail without me, and then catch her up at Cyprus by means of the Khedival mail-boat *Kosseir*. On shore I had to interview any number of likely 'agents', or rather people who thought they were likely. As a matter of fact good agents were very few and far between, and my experience taught me that while most of them were very brave in Port Said, it was only one in a hundred who was worth a damn when once at sea. But after a while I did not put into Port Said as often as I had used to do. For, as our troops had advanced into Palestine, Jaffa was often more convenient, although there is no harbour there, and even the anchorage is dangerous when there is any sea running, on account of a number of half-submerged reefs.

It was while I was in Jaffa for the first time (in April) that I managed to arrange a trip, half for duty and half for pleasure, to

Jerusalem. I had to make the journey by motor lorry and Ford car; and, beautiful as Palestine is in the spring months, what I chiefly remember is the dust. I was nearly dead of suffocation when I reached the Holy City, and I was also thoroughly nerve- racked, for the Ford had tackled the hair-pin bends on the mountain road without (I thought) slackening its speed. My driver must have been a man of iron.

I had arranged to join the *Managem* at Port Said; and so, after spending a few days at the Governorate, I left with Edmunds, of the EMSIB, to visit GHQ, which was then at Bir Salem, close to Ramleh. Here, for the first time, I met my OC, Colonel Deeds; and also Major Woods, who was commonly known as 'Bosphorus Bill', as he hailed from Constantinople. After Colonel Deeds had been most complimentary, and had told me that General Allenby wanted to see me the next time I was there, I pushed off and caught the Kantara train. At Kantara I had to change and, whilst waiting for the Port Said train, I committed something in the nature of a *faux pas*. I was standing on the platform, when I heard someone call my name. I turned round and exclaimed, 'Hullo, Hoskins! How are you? I haven't seen you for years.' Then I suddenly realised that I was speaking to a Major-General, who was surrounded by his Staff. (Of course, I saluted and apologised.) It was General Hoskins, late C-in-C, East Africa, who had been taking a look round the Palestine front. When I knew him before in 1908 he had been Major Hoskins, on the Staff in Cairo.

It was a few days after my return from Palestine to Port Said that I ran into old Abdulla, the senior of my boatmen. Some weeks earlier I had dispensed with his services and those of his three sons, and he had bought himself a small schooner. He told me that while coming from Cyprus on his last trip, he had been stopped by a German submarine, which, after ordering the crew into their boats, had sunk his little ship. He had had a long row in, but it was extremely lucky for him that the Huns had not made him a prisoner and taken him with them to Beirut, where he would almost certainly have been recognised – and hanged.

At the end of April the *Veresis*, Salter's trawler, was taken from us by the Admiral and replaced by the *Devany*. This latter ship did not impress me a bit when I saw her. She was of about 600 tons, and years before the war had been run – as the *Devonia* – between Plymouth and the French coast. She could only knock up about 8 knots at the best. I felt very sick about her. What we really wanted was a fast yacht, and I had repeatedly applied for one. This was the result.

On the 4th May, I put out to sea again in the *Managem*, taking with me an agent whom I intended to land in the vicinity of Ras el Nakura, a headland a few miles north of Acre. And land him I did on the following night.

The landing-place was ideal for our sort of work. One rushed through the surf, then shot (one had to make a good shot) between two rocks, and arrived in a tiny little cove in which the sea was absolutely calm. Later I came here several times and, even when the surf was bad, was nearly always able to land. It was a spot from which, before the war, Syrians who were going to be conscripted for the Turkish army used to be taken off – at a price – by small schooners, which used then to stand out to sea, intercept some passing foreign steamer, and put on board their 'wild geese', who were carried on to Port Said and Alexandria. In fact, it was a regular smuggler's cove, for in the piping times of peace, salt used to be landed there from Port Said and taken away by camels into the interior. (I need hardly mention that there had never been a custom-house in this port!) I was lucky enough to have among my boatmen a Syrian who had formerly been the skipper of a schooner engaged in this trade, and his knowledge of the place was very useful to me.

Four days later (8th May) we put back to Nakura, to pick up the agent I had landed. I went ashore, and after I had waited for an hour or so he turned up, bringing with him the man whom I had sent him to fetch. This latter was the 'big bug' of a certain district inland, and I spent a couple of hours under a rock talking to him. I explained what I wanted him to do for us, and then presented him with a rifle, a pair of binoculars, some coffee and some sugar. After this things proceeded very smoothly and, having appointed a date for our next meeting, I returned to the boat, taking with me the agent and his wife and child, whom I had promised to take out of the country if he did his job properly.

Henceforward we used Nakura as one of our regular landing-stations. We were very glad to have it; for, as I have said, Athlit had been raided by the enemy, and Tyre we had overworked. About this time the Turks must have smelt a rat; a rat which they very nearly succeeded in catching. For one night (the 2nd July) when I was at Nakura waiting for an agent, I suddenly saw a large party making towards me. They were scarcely more than 150 yards away when I spotted them; and, although there was no moon, it was a clear starlit night. Luckily, I was in the boat and not actually on shore, as I had been only a few minutes earlier. I lost no time in giving the order to push off. A few shots were fired at us, and one of my boatmen called to his fellows to pull lying down. Of course, they couldn't pull in that position – it was hopeless – so I made them sit up and pull properly; after which I turned my attention to the Lewis gun – how thankful I was we had one! – and let fly a few rounds. The enemy disappeared, and we got safely away. But it had been a near thing.

It was just after this little episode that another trouble cropped up – my agents began to get nervy and wanted to throw in their hands. Most of them, however, I managed to persuade to keep going for a little longer. But one fellow let me down badly. I had put him ashore at Nakura to bring a man I knew of ashore to meet me at the landing-place on a certain night; but when on the arranged date I landed, I found only my agent and no friend. The agent assured me that he had done his job, and that the other man would not come to the rendezvous as he thought it too dangerous. But I was sure he was lying, and after cross-examining him I came to the conclusion that he had never taken my message at all; but that, after he had landed, he had simply lain hidden close to the shore and waited there for me to pick him up again.

This failure was most annoying, as it meant that I should have to arrange means of getting into touch with my friends ashore all over again. Accordingly, I sailed for Famagusta, and there set one of my boatmen quietly to work to try and find a really trustworthy messenger who knew our agent on the other side and would be willing to land and take him a message. The boatman returned to the ship in the evening and said he knew of a man, but at that moment he was a prisoner in Famagusta gaol. Apparently he was one of the crew of a Turkish schooner that had been captured by a French patrol-boat on the Syrian coast a month or two before.

I obtained permission from the Commandant of Police to visit the gaol, and saw six men. The minute they saw me they fell on their knees, clasped me round the legs and began kissing my boots. They implored me to have mercy on them and set them free. The reason for their terror (I discovered afterwards) was, that I happened to be standing at the door of the building in which the gallows was and they thought I was some high official who was making up his mind which he would hang! I did not speak to the man I wanted in front of the others, but later in the evening he was brought down to the ship. He agreed to act as my messenger if I promised that, when fetching him off-shore again, I would allow him to bring with him his wife and child, who, he said, naturally thought he was dead and were most likely starving. This I agreed to do, paid him well, and arranged that if he played the game he should not be put back into prison on our return to Cyprus. Then, having thus fixed things pretty well to my satisfaction, we sailed for Nakura.

Landing our new recruit was easy enough. What troubled me was the job of picking him up again; for, if he took it into his head to betray us, he could arrange for our capture without the slightest difficulty: and I knew little or nothing about him. But I had to take the risk, and on the evening of the 15th July we steamed in towards the land. At midnight I got into the boat and was rowed to the beach.

When running through the surf into the little cove I must confess that I was in a blue funk. If he had 'played me false' – as the villain is generally supposed to do in novels – there was no turning back, and we were 'for it'. We ran in all right, however, and accompanied by my head man I crawled on shore to the rendezvous, taking with me a revolver and a loaded cane. No one was there, so we concealed ourselves behind some rocks and awaited events. After about an hour, during which time I must have seen at least one thousand Turks (purely imaginary) creeping up to collar me, we spied two figures, who cautiously came down to the rendezvous – a large rock – and sat down. We approached them, and my man called out something, which was answered. He then walked towards them, and as it was evidently 'OK' I followed. Here we found the man with whom I had been trying to get into touch, and our new agent. All was well. I spent about two hours sitting under that rock, explaining in bad Arabic what I wanted our friend to do for us, and – this certainly interested him a great deal more – what we would do for him in return. 'And so to ship,' as Mr Pepys might have said.

Cain had gone home on leave a month or so earlier, his place being taken by Captain Smith, of the *Veresis*; and while he was away a real tragedy occurred on board.

One morning poor old 'Paddy' – Cain's bulldog – could not be found. He had evidently slipped overboard during the night while chasing rats. His loss cast a gloom over the whole ship's company, with all of whom he was a special favourite. One of the men went as far as to say to me, 'He never *fell* overboard, sir! He had more sense. He could do everything except talk' – and then the man cried. He was insinuating that some man who had been punished had pushed Paddy over, out of spite. None of us believed, however, that we had a man on the ship who would have done such a thing, bad character or not. What worried us most was the thought of poor old Paddy paddling about and barking for the ship to wait for him – as it certainly would if we had only heard him: and he was an excellent swimmer. We wondered what Cain, his owner, would think when we informed him of his loss. As a matter of fact, some months later, when Cain returned from leave, he told me that one night when he was leaving a theatre in Liverpool he heard loud shouts of 'Captain Cain! Captain Cain!' and saw an excited Bluejacket fighting his way through the crowd towards him. When the sailor reached him, he said, 'Have yer heard about the loss of Paddy?' It was our bos'n, who had gone home on leave after the loss, had spotted Cain, and felt impelled to break the news.

17

Nearing the End

August–October, 1918

MORE OFFICE WORK in Port Said, more trips in the *Managem*, more agents, more landings, more talks with 'friends' ashore! These, if I wrote them down, would make up the tale of the next two months. But I am not going to write them down. The reader who has been staunch enough to struggle so far deserves a little consideration and, not being a professional writer, I will give him his due. At least I will try not to bore him (or her?) more than I have done already.

Early in August we happened to be lying in Famagusta harbour, when the *Devany* came in and anchored fairly close to us. She had, as it appeared, had quite an interesting experience on the Asia Minor coast. One day, when not far from the shore, she spotted a man come down to the beach, wade into the water, and wave a white rag. At once a boat was lowered and sent to pick him up. This it did – not without being fired at by some Turks on land. The *Devany*, however, sent over a few shells, and the boat got back in safety. The man who had been picked up turned out to be an Indian soldier of the 24th Punjabis. He had been taken prisoner at Kut el Amara, and after many hard marches had been put to work – with about twelve other Indians – repairing the telegraph line on the road that ran along the coast from Mersina to Selefkeh. He told me later that he had seen the ship and suggested to his companions that they should crawl down to the shore, when the guards were not looking, and get taken off. The other prisoners said, 'No, it might not be a British ship'; but he insisted that it was sure to be one, as there were only British ships on the sea! The others, however, wouldn't risk it: so he went off alone, and was justified by the result. The first thing he asked me for was a uniform – he was in rags and was as pleased as Punch when I gave him a pair of shorts, puttees and an old tunic. He told me that the Turks had treated the Mohammedan Indian prisoners very well, but the poor British Tommy very badly.

Up to this time, although I myself was GSI., I had received all my orders through the EMSIB. But in the middle of August, when I happened to be spending a few days in Jerusalem, I was informed that the latter department was shutting up shop. In fact, I saw Edmunds, who told me that he was going home. For this I was very sorry, as Edmunds was a most capable man and a charming fellow in every way, and had done an immense amount of valuable work. I may say here that all he got for his services was an OBE, which everyone who knew anything about his work looked upon as quite inadequate.

Towards the end of the month I did another of my little landings at Nakura, and had a chat with my friend the 'big bug' from the interior. On this occasion he asked me to tell the C-in-C that if he (the C-in-C) wished, he would lead sixty thousand of his armed tribesmen to attack Acre and Haifa from the north, while the British attacked from the south. I communicated this offer to GHQ, and was told to thank my friend and to do my best to keep him and his men quiet.

On 12th September, Cain, our Captain, returned from leave. I was especially glad to see him as he gave me a lot of news about my wife and family, whom I had not seen since 1914. He had very kindly paid them a visit in Ireland and told them all – or a good deal – about what I was doing. Of course, I had been unable to give them particulars through the post.

We now heard that eight British officers, who had escaped from a Turkish prisoners of war camp in Asia Minor, had arrived in Cyprus. On the evening of the 16th September I was sent for by the SNO, Captain Betts, who told me that he wanted me, with Smith (late of the *Veresis*), to go on board a French destroyer and proceed at full speed to Cyprus and then to the Gulf of Adalia on the Asia Minor coast. News had been received that another party of escaped prisoners were expected shortly on that coast, and we were to try and rescue them. Next morning *Veresis* Smith and I sailed in the French torpedo-boat destroyer *Arbalette*. The captain, Millot by name, was a charming man and looked after us well. The motion of the torpedo-boat destroyer was not nearly so bad as that of the *Managem*, even in a bad sea. We arrived next morning at Famagusta, and at once went off to the RNO's office – 'Kiss me, Hardy', was now RNO – and reported. Here we met Lieut.-Commander Cochrane, DSO, who had been the leader of the escaped prisoners.

It was arranged that *Veresis* Smith should go on to the Gulf of Adalia at once in the torpedo-boat destroyer, and that I was to remain and collect all the information that Cochrane had to give us. I should have mentioned before this that we had been warned to be on the look out for British prisoners at a certain place near Seefkeh, and that we had run up there in the *Devany* and *Managem*, but had seen nothing.

Cochrane now told me that in 1915 he had been in command of Submarine E 7, operating in the Dardanelles and Sea of Marmora. In fact, his was one of the two submarines I had seen there when I was up at Gallipoli. Apparently, when going up the Straits one day, he got caught in the Turkish nets. As soon as the Turks noticed that something was in the nets, they guessed it was a submarine, and started to locate it by sounding. Cochrane said he could hear the lead bumping on top of the submarine's deck. Then the Turks dropped two bombs or depth-charges, which disabled the submarine, but also freed her from the net, and she popped up on the surface. Cochrane managed to destroy the submarine to prevent her falling into the enemy's hands, and then landed his crew, who were all promptly taken prisoners. He himself escaped in 1917 from his prison camp – I forget where it was – but was recaptured, shut up in a filthy gaol, and after some time sent off to the big prisoners of war camp at Yozgod, situated about 300 miles north-east of Mersina. In 1918 he and seven others, Indian army officers and one RE, managed to escape. They had been able to inform London that they were going to make the attempt, and had asked for a ship to be on the look out for them between certain dates. This, as I mentioned previously, we had arranged. After a terrible march of over 300 miles across the mountains, with many hair-breadth escapes, the party arrived on the sea coast at Khorghos, absolutely worn out and starving. They were so done in and weak that they were unable to keep a proper look out and so missed us.

After they had recovered a little, they saw a motor boat towing a barge down the coast. She came in and anchored in a little cove just below them. At once they determined to try and steal her. That night they went down and swam out to the boat. There was luckily no one on board, so they carefully hoisted up the anchor, got out two oars that were in the boat, and noiselessly paddled her out of the cove. Once safely outside, they tried to start the engine, but at first without success, and they were beginning to think that all was over, when it suddenly began to run. Cochrane took the helm and steered for Cyprus, about ninety miles away. On looking round they found that there was not much petrol on board, and prayed that there might be enough to hold out. Actually, it was exhausted when they were within a few hundred yards of safety – in the shape of the Cyprus coast near Kyrenia. They had, however, been seen: moreover, Cochrane swam ashore and explained. So eventually they were taken into Kyrenia, and their troubles were at an end.

I may mention here that Smith was not successful in his attempt to find the other party of escaped prisoners. In fact he had been unable to find the rendezvous, which had been described to us somewhat vaguely as 'two big, peculiar-shaped rocks in a bay'.

We returned to Egypt from this ship on September 22nd and were greeted with the splendid news of General Allenby's victory, which we immediately celebrated with a pleasant little dinner – Cochrane, Cain, Lieut. de Vaisseau Riccard, of the *Nord Capper*, and myself. It was a victory with special results for Cain and myself, and on the 3rd October we began to realise them.

We were just going to sail for Nakura when we received a signal saying that Captains Cain and Weldon were wanted at Navy House. Off we went, and on arriving were told that the Admiral (he was at Ismailia) wanted to speak to us urgently on the telephone. We each took a receiver, and the Admiral started off telling us that he was about to give us important orders. These were as follows:

The *Managem* was to sail at once, first for Es-Surr and thence on to Saida and Beirut. At each place the ship was to lie off the shore and a boat was to be sent in to find out if the Turks were still in occupation of the town or if they had evacuated. The Admiral then said, 'All the landings are to be made by Captain Weldon.' He chuckled, and then added, 'He'll like that[?]. He will know if the Turks are still there, as they are sure to fire if they are.' Pleasant! Then, after visiting each place, we were to send a wireless and, if possible, come down to the coast and report to our advancing troops. So back we went, quite excited at having something new to do, and sailed at once.

On the way we put into Haifa, which our troops had already occupied. Here we found twelve trawlers and numerous ships carrying stores for the Army. The next morning we were off again, taking a motor launch with us as escort, and arrived off Surr at 10 a.m.

Just as I was going ashore we saw a number of our cavalry ride into the place, and when I landed I found the Herts Yeomanry in possession and a Major Gordon, of the London Yeomanry, already appointed commandant. My boatmen, who, as I said before, all came from here, were at once seized on by their friends, and I also was introduced. I had often visited the place during the previous two years, but only at night, and would have liked to explore it; but we had our orders and could not afford the time. So with great difficulty, having got my boat's crew together again, I went back to the ship and sailed for Saida (Sidon).

On the way we stopped a schooner and found she had left Beirut a few days before. The crew said the Turks were there when they left. I asked them if the Bay of Beirut was mined – a report had said that it was. The captain of the schooner said 'No,' but added that he advised us to hug the shore when going in. I didn't like to trust him as he was a Turk, so I took him on board and told him that if we were blown up he would share our fate. We then ordered the schooner to sail into Tyre and give herself up (and this she did), and proceeded gaily on our way. We arrived off Sidon at 3p.m. the same day. Having placed the Lewis gun in the stem-sheets of the boat, and taking rifles and a revolver with me, I pushed off for shore. When we got close to the harbour I could see that the whole quay was packed with people (as were also the roofs of the houses), who when we drew near started to wave, shout and clap their hands. Apparently there were no Turks, so I rowed up to the quay and stepped on shore.

The people were wild with excitement and seized hold of me, kissing my hands and even my boots. The only danger I was in was of getting a ducking by being pushed into the sea by people pressing from behind. To escape this I jumped back into my boat, and half a dozen inhabitants jumped in with me. One of these then stood up and made me a speech, in which he said he welcomed me in the name of the Cherif of Mecca, and pointed to the Cherifian flag which was flying over the town. Apparently what had happened was that the Turkish garrison had been withdrawn the day before we arrived, and the Arabs, of whom my friend was one, had declared for the Cherif of Mecca, he himself being appointed Governor. This he told me, and then called for cheers, firstly, for myself; secondly, for the Cherif of Mecca; and thirdly, for the King of England. I am not unduly modest, but I felt distinctly shy in such distinguished company. An elderly gentleman in a straw hat and black tail-coat now turned up. He introduced himself to me as Dr George Ford, an American missionary, who lived there. He was charming, and I got him to make a short speech on my behalf, thanking the people for their kind reception. With his help also I informed the self-appointed Governor that the British troops would be arriving outside the town next day, adding that I was sure the General would be pleased if he would meet him, point out where the troops could camp, and have water ready for the horses.

At last – a long last – I managed to tear myself out of the crowd and return to the ship. Once on board, we headed south along the coast until we spotted our cavalry coming up from Surr. I went away in the boat to meet them, and informed the OC, a Colonel Tyrrell, of the 5th Irish Lancers, of what I had learnt. After this we returned northwards once more and made for Beirut. On the whole I had spent an exciting, triumphant and tiring day.

It was just dawn on 6th October when we arrived off Ras el Beirut. We had made up our minds that it would be too risky to take the ship through a possible minefield into the bay, and I was just about to get into my boat when we spotted dense smoke on the southern horizon. Naturally we were very keen on being the first Allied ship to sail into Beirut harbour, so Cain and I held a hurried palaver. I explained that as far as I was concerned I would like the *Managem* to go in: but I pointed out that after all he was the Captain, and so responsible for the safety of his ship. If anything happened it would be his pigeon. For a moment he hesitated, and then said, 'Oh, damn it; we'll risk it!' So away we went at full speed.

All the crew were ordered to put on their lifebelts, but I felt that if we did bump a mine there would not be much left of the 160-ton *Managem*, and that a parachute would possibly meet the case better than a lifebelt.

The ships behind us were two French TBDs which came tearing along after us at 22 knots, and we were just entering the bay when they caught us up. They then slowed down and followed us in, and we all arrived safely off the mouth of the harbour.

The whole of the breakwaters and quays were black with people waving and shouting.

I rowed in in my boat, and the Frenchmen steamed alongside the quay and tied up in the very place where only a few days before one German and one Austrian submarine had moored. The French captain – my old friend of the *Arbalète* – and I then had a talk with the harbour master, who told us that the Turkish troops had evacuated the town the day before and had departed inland. He also pointed out to us the portions of the bay that were not mined

– we knew one of them – and said that the town had declared for the Cherif of Mecca. Later, he asked us to drive through the town in a carriage surrounded by a mounted escort, to receive the acclamations of the populace! The Frenchman looked at me to see what I would say. I replied that I was very small fry, and had only been sent with orders to find out if the Turks had left, and, having done so, must return at once and report to our advancing troops. The harbour master next turned and asked the Frenchman, who tactfully replied that his orders were identical with mine.

The French destroyers steamed out and sailed for Port Said, and I rowed back to the *Managem* amid cheers. By this time a band had turned out, and was doing its best with 'God save the King!' Nor was our little triumph yet over. For I had hardly got on board and told Cain what I had done, when a whole boatload of notables arrived and came into the saloon. They presented me with a letter of welcome from the self-appointed Governor. I replied, thanking them, and said I would take the letter down the coast and hand it to the OC of the advancing troops, and that I hoped he would shortly arrive and be able to thank them in person. I asked them to have camping grounds and water prepared. They then tried to persuade us to steam the *Managem* round the harbour – now that the French had left – so that the people might see and welcome properly the British flag. Cain and I refused as we thought it might be impolite. So we showed them to their boat and sailed.

We were all very pleased with ourselves, as we had the satisfaction of knowing that we were the first British ship to go into Beirut since the war began.

We returned to Saida, and I went on shore and found our troops camped just outside the town.

This time I had yet another royal reception, and marched through the town with a priest on one side of me and the Acting- Governor on the other, each of them holding tightly to one of my hands.

18

Conclusion

To CARRY MY narrative any further would be to risk an anti-climax. Certainly our work was not yet entirely finished, and for another month or so we were kept at it, doing odd jobs for the French on the Asia Minor coast. For a time we went on making our landings just as of old, while 'information' still kept trickling in to be combed out and reported. But all such last activities of ours seemed tame after our triumphal flying visits to the Syrian ports. They were the morning after the champagne supper, so to speak, and as such deserve no place in a volume of war stories. So, as far as I am able, I consign them to oblivion.

But of the last struggle of all I must speak. That, at least, I shall never forget. Yet it did not occur until after I had closed down my Port Said office, visited GHQ, and put my clearance certificate into my breast pocket. In fact it did not start until January, 1919, when I found myself at the Transit Camp with my name 1,371st on the waiting list for a passage home. But then I hurled myself into the fray and fought with unparalleled enthusiasm. Also, I made an ally of a man in a shipping office – and with his help I conquered. It was still January when I sailed for England. If I took with me but little luggage, I took also the memory of a splendid comradeship.

Appendix

Sir Robert Paul's Letter from Turkish Prison

Constantinople,
26th November, 1915.

My Dear Weldon,

Thanks awfully for sending me the medicine. I suppose it was you who sent it, though there was nothing to say from where it came.

Langly sent me some money, which was very good of him. Will you tell him how awfully grateful I am to him in case he did not get the letter I wrote him.

I am quite well, and being well treated.

I was taken prisoner owing to the engine of the aeroplane failing on the way back from following a line to a town in Syria, where I had gone to do reconnaissance. Everything had gone well, and we had just turned for home when the engine started to weaken, though nothing to frighten us at first. However, it soon got worse, and when we were about twelve miles from the coast we had to come down. My pilot, a Frenchman named Trouillet, made a magnificent landing without upsetting. The only pity was we came down among a crowd of Arabs, who were on to us in a minute, before we had time to set light to the machine. However, the Arabs proceeded to smash it up pretty effectively, as they explained afterwards to the Turkish officers, they were afraid of it getting up and flying off on its own!!

The Arabs gave us a bad time for a bit, and took our clothing, watches and cigarette-cases, etc. I offered them £200 to help us to escape, but it was no use. In the afternoon another aeroplane from the ship flew over us, no doubt coming to look for us. We spent the day with the Arabs. Trouillet had been taken in one direction and I in another.

About eight in the evening three Turkish officers, two lieutenants and an aviation officer, arrived from the town over which we had flown in the morning to take us back there. I cannot say too much for the kindness of these officers. They returned all our property that the Arabs took from us, and gave us coats and food, mounted us on fine riding camels, and about 10 p.m. we started off southwards. Towards daybreak we arrived at the town, and just as we were arriving my camel took fright at some trucks and I fell off, but was not hurt a bit.

When we arrived the officers took us to their tents, gave us hot tea, whisky and food, and afterwards a suit of pyjamas and camp-beds. In fact they did all they could for us while we were with them. Three days later we were taken by carriage to Jerusalem and thence by rail to Damascus and Constantinople. Trouillet and I have not been separated, and we have all we need, and are being very well treated.

Happy Christmas to you and all my pals.

(Signed)
Yours ever,
R. J. PAUL.

Biographical Afterword

L EWEN WELDON ALWAYS defined himself as an Irishman, though he was born in England on 15 October 1875, the fourth child of Rev. Lewen Burton Weldon, vicar of Holy Trinity, Weymouth. But the reverend had grown up in Ireland, one of the eleven children of Sir Anthony Weldon of Rahenderry, County Kildare. Lewen's mother, Olivia Maria Barrington, was also Irish: one of the daughters of Sir Croker Barrington from Limerick. It was typical of such Anglo-Irish families that the eldest son inherited the land and the younger brothers sought employment in one of the professions, typically either in the Church, the military or the colonial administration.

Lewen was educated at St Edward's School in Oxford, then at Trinity College, Dublin with the long summer holidays spent with his Irish uncles and doing some useful work experience at Lord Wimborne's estate office in Dorset. After university he took the stiffly competitive exam for the Egyptian Civil Service and having won a place, was posted to the Survey Department. Lewen first went out to Egypt in 1901 as a 26-year-old, travelling on the *Cheshire*, one of the ships of the Bibby Line. He would travel twenty-two times as a passenger with the Bibby Line and was delighted by each journey. As the son of a clergyman, money had always been tight, so travelling from Tilbury to Port Said seemed to be just one continuous party, all for a £12 first-class ticket.

When Lewen arrived, the Egyptian Civil Service was still under the autocratic direction of Lord Cromer, 'whose guiding principle was to take infinite care to procure the best mean for any given job of work and then to let him get on with it'. Lord Cromer was efficient, incorruptible and imperious but as the living representative of the

British Empire's dominance over Egypt he was also loathed. The Ministry of Finance, the Ministry of Public Works and the Irrigation Department maintained government rest houses in all the principal towns, whilst the Ministry of Interior had rooms in the more important police stations. However the Survey of Egypt were tent-dwellers, constantly sent out on *maroor* – inspection duty. Lewen cut his teeth working in the delta, helping complete a 6-inch Ordnance Survey map for this densely populated, flat and fertile region. There was no such thing as uncultivated space in the delta, so the surveyors got used to pitching their tent on the village threshing ground, which normally stood beside the murky, mosquito-friendly waters of the village brick pit. Lewen worked from dawn to dusk, mucking in with village life or in a more isolated camp 'splitting a tin of sardines, washed down by tea and ideal milk'. This healthy, spartan life was broken by time off in Cairo. Social life for expatriate civil servants was dominated by four hotels each with its own nickname: Shephard's with Notoriety, Savoy with Society, Continental with Variety and Angleterre with Propriety. In terms of charm, none matched The Mena House and The Gezira – old palaces of Khedive Ismail Pasha that had been converted to hotels. Lewen's zest for life was quickly recognised and he was placed in charge of the annual St Patrick's Day Ball, complete with indoor shinty matches after dinner.

After two years working in the delta, Lewen was sent to Nubia (southernmost Egypt, upstream of Aswan). In 1907 he went even further south, to work on the upper waters of the Nile, calculating river volumes below Murchison's Falls, and fine- tuning the seasonal difference in levels between Lake Victoria and Lake Albert. Rather than proceeding up the Nile, Lewen's survey team reached the East African headwaters of the Nile by marching inland from the Somali shore.

The success of this mission led to Lewen being asked to join a survey of Northern Sinai on behalf of the War Office. His colleagues in this task were two very keen young officers, King from the Royal Engineers and Pitt-Taylor, seconded from the Rifle Brigade. Lewen assessed that it would take six years to produce a full survey of the Sinai mountains, so they cut to the quick of their brief which was to look at the Turkish frontier forts and the best routes by which an army might engage with them. It was confidential work which brought him into contact with the two charismatic British officers who policed this mountain region, Parker Pasha and Beamish Bey. Lewen's energy, professional competence and ebullient charm had once again been noticed, alongside his skill with languages and his ability to work with any team of men, of whatever race, religion or class.

In 1911 Lewen hitched a lift in the first British submarine travelling underwater through the Suez Canal. He described it as a lark, but he was also possibly interested in working out effective measures against enemy submarines doing this in time of war. He was then sent back to Sinai to lead his own survey team, looking at possible rail routes, should a British army advance into southern Syria and need to be supplied from Egypt. In the summer of 1914, before war broke out and on his own initiative, Lewen collected together a dossier on all the freshwater wells in the deserts of Egypt. Discreet observation of these wells would enable the British to track any foreign intelligence service operating in the area.

On the outbreak of the First World War, Lewen was seconded to the Intelligence Department formed by Gilbert Clayton, who assembled a small team with some impressive hands-on experience of the various landscape and peoples of the Near East. Lewen shared a suite of rooms with George Lloyd, Leonard Wooley, Aubrey Herbert, David Hogarth, T. E. Lawrence and Stewart 'Skinface' Newcombe. One of the early problems of this Intelligence Department was that they found themselves serving three rival masters: Generals Maxwell, Murray and Altham of, respectively, the Mediterranean Expeditionary Force, the Levant Base, and Egyptian Command.

Hard Lying describes most of Lewen's activities between 1914– 18 as he witnessed them. He does not record the work of his colleagues but was always conscious that his amphibian work was balanced by an additional stream of land-based intelligence provided by Parker Pasha, who had infiltrated the desert frontier. As you will have discovered, he first commanded the SS *Aenne Rickmers*, a German cargo-boat, which had been seized and converted into a 'transport auxiliary', the HMTA *Anne*. By August 1915 she had been converted into one of the first aircraft carriers. The upgraded HMS *Anne* sailed under the White Ensign as one of the Royal Naval Air Service's seaplane tenders, equipped with two-seater Nieuport VI floatplanes. Lewen observed the initial Gallipoli landings aboard HMS *Euryalus*.

In January 1916, Weldon was informed by his colleagues in Cairo that 'they had procured a yacht for the spy business'. By the spring of 1916, Weldon was in charge of HMY *Managem*, which delivered spies into Ottoman Turkish territory. Weldon had strong Arabic, which allowed him to debrief agents on board or row himself to shore for night-time meetings, to land agents, keep them supplied and to pick them up at the end of their mission. The *Managem* was skippered by Lt-Cdr Alan Cain RNR, 'a first-class man, a real stout-hearted fellow. He had been in "sail" first but just before the war, had been the skipper of a New Zealand Union Steamship Co. Steamer.'

At the end of the war, Lewen Weldon was awarded the Military Cross, 'for an unusual combination of service on land and sea'. In 1919 he returned to his old job and was quickly promoted to become Surveyor-General of Egypt (1919–23). It was a confusing period for British officials. The Egyptians had been infuriated by the British refusal to allow Saad Pasha Zaghloul to attend the post-war peace conference. Nationalist street demonstrations erupted in all the big Egyptian cities, backed by armed rebellions in some provinces. British authority was eventually re-established but only at the cost of hundreds of Egyptian casualties, shot dead on the streets.

The British realised that they had seriously misjudged the national mood and that nothing short of a permanent military garrison could now uphold their unpopular domination. Since this would be too expensive, liberal-looking commissions of inquiry were launched and negotiations with selected nationalists paved the way for a new understanding. Egypt would acquire a parliamentary constitution under the hereditary monarchy of the Khedives and a new status within the British Empire. The declaration of 1922 formally ended the political and fiscal powers of the British protectorate, but they kept control over the military, the canal, the national frontiers and foreign policy.

Many Arab nationalists were not certain what had been won by these negotiations, and if they looked east over Palestine, Iraq, Jordan and the Emirates along the Persian Gulf, the authority of the British Empire appeared to be expanding not contracting. For their part, the British retreated into a garrison mentality within Egypt. It was almost as if they could never quite forget the Beni Mazar incident of 1919, when seven British passengers had been dragged from a train and lynched. This lingering sense of threat was reinforced by periodic assassinations by the nationalists.

In 1923 Lewen tendered his resignation and took formal leave of King Fuad in the Montaza Palace. The King was too much of an Egyptian nationalist to ever want to speak English in public, but his Arabic (Turkish was his native tongue) was not as good as Lewen's. So the two men chatted in bad French, sharing a pride in what had been achieved by the Survey of Egypt.

The revolution in Egypt had been mirrored by a similar struggle that had transformed the political realities within Lewen's Irish homeland. The long agitation for Irish Home Rule had almost been peacefully resolved, but the First World War battened down the hatches on reform. This delay had catastrophic consequences. The suppression of the 1916 Easter Uprising polarised the nation and the struggle continued with greater earnestness after the war. The armed struggle for independence ended only with the unpopular compromise peace, which left the northern quarter of Ireland (Ulster) as part of the United Kingdom. A divisive and bloody civil war, between pro- and anti-peace treaty parties, was inevitable. Many Anglo-Irish families decided to leave Ireland or already had that decision made for them, when they were burned out of their grand old houses.

Although Lewen was a senior official within the British Empire, his sense of his Irish identity had never been in doubt and had been further confirmed by his marriage to Mary Macaulay Molloy. Far from being descended from a Cromwellian settler, like so many of Lewen's Anglo-Irish ancestors, his wife's family, the O'Molloys of Firceall, had been in possession of their lands since the 4th century.

Lewen returned home (by boat of course) to Clonbeale House, Birr, County Offally, to help his wife look after her estate. He died in 1958 and was survived by his only child, Olivia Mary, better known as Molly. Olivia Mary never married and in the 1960s decided to sell up and move to Dorset. She left her father's papers and literary estate to her favourite cousin Bridget, who was a young art student – now a renowned sculptor – interested in Middle Eastern archaeology. Bridget married Robert McCrum, who rose to become a submarine captain in the Royal Navy. He was my father's oldest friend, both having joined up as ten-year-old naval cadets in 1940. After the deaths of these two naval officers, I used to entertain my mother and two of her widowed friends by organising an annual journey in the dull month of February, exploring different parts of the Western Desert of Egypt in a small convoy of jeeps. We had lots of time to chat, and it was here that I first heard about the work of Bridget's great uncle, Lewen Weldon. My interest encouraged Bridget to give me a rare copy of *Hard Lying* and after I expressed interest in it, she lent me his unpublished diaries, the source for this biographical note.

Barnaby Rogerson
London, 2023

ELAND

61 Exmouth Market, London EC1R 4QL
Email: info@travelbooks.co.uk

Eland was started in 1982 to revive great travel books which had fallen out of print. Although the list soon diversified into biography and fiction, all the titles are chosen for their interest in spirit of place. One of our readers explained that for him reading an Eland is like listening to an experienced anthropologist at the bar – she's let her hair down and is telling all the stories that were just too good to go into the textbook.

Eland books are for travellers, and for those who are content to travel in their own minds. We can never quite define what we are looking for, but they need to be observant of others, to catch the moment and place on the wing and to have a page-turning gift for storytelling. And they might do that while being, by turns, funny, wry, intelligent, humane, universal, self-deprecating and idiosyncratic. We take immense trouble to select only the most readable books and therefore many people collect the entire series.

Extracts from each and every one of our books can be read on our website, at www.travelbooks.co.uk. If you would like a free copy of our catalogue, please order it from the website, email us or send a postcard.